The Hermetica 101

A modern, practical guide, plain and simple

by Matthew S. Barnes

Also By Matthew Barnes

1. **Ancient Egyptian Enlightenment Series:**
   (amazon.com/author/matthewbarnes)
   The Emerald Tablet 101
   The Hermetica 101
   The Kybalion 101
2. **The Zen-nish Series:**
   (amazon.com/author/matthewbarnes)
   The Tao Te Ching 101
   Albert Einstein, Zen Master
   The Tao Te Ching 201
   Jesus Christ, Zen Master
   Dr. Seuss, Zen Master
3. **The Hindu Enlightenment Series:**
   The Bhagavad Gita 101
4. **Investing Series (Zen-vesting)**
   (amazon.com/author/matthewbarnes)
   Investing 101
   Investing 201
5. **Novels**
   (amazon.com/author/msbarnes)
   Folie¿ (a creepy, psychological thriller)
   Meet Frank King (psychological thriller)

DEDICATION

I'd like to dedicate this book to my parents.

I have great parents. They have always been very good to me. They have always been very supportive of everything that I have tried to do, have always been there when things didn't work out the way that I wanted them to, and they have always been quick to tell me that they were proud of me.

Additionally, I feel like I received my more scientific side from my father, who is more matter-of-fact. I received a degree in Biochemistry and Chemistry from NC State due to my curiosities in science, which seems to reflect my dad's input.

On the other hand, I believe I received my curiosities into religion and related subjects from my mom. I can't even begin to tell you how many hours I have spent and how many books I have read on religious, philosophical and spiritual subjects. It is another area of burning interest and curiosities for me, and an area of interest I feel I inherited from my mom.

I feel this book is an overall mirror of how I see the relationships between science and religion. As this book will explain: "Religion is the Study of God. Science is the study of what God created." I believe this to my core.

I'd also like to dedicate this book to Robin, who has struggled her entire life with the existential question of "why"- why are we here? What is our purpose? Maybe this book has a few answers.

I believe we are all searching for the same answers to the same questions: What is Life? What is this world? Why are we here? And so on. Some of us are more comfortable searching for these answers through science, some through religion. I believe we are all studying the same thing, just coming at it from different angles. In this book, both viewpoints seem to merge, or at least it did for me.

CONTENTS

INTRODUCTION

The Kybalion, the Hermetica and the Emerald Tablet are a few of the main, core writings putting forth the ancient Egyptian philosophy of life, what creates life, what our purpose is here on earth and what is beyond this life. In general, these writings are referred to as "Hermetic"- the philosophy is named after its creator, Hermes.

Originally, I tried to combine all the Hermetic information into one book, but it was too cumbersome. In order to make digesting the information easier, I have chosen to explain the Hermetic teachings in three separate works- "The Hermetica 101", "The Kybalion 101" and "The Emerald Tablet 101".

Like the Tao Te Ching, the first book I wrote about (*The Wisdom and Peace of the Teachings of the Tao Te Ching*), the Hermetica is attributed to the authorship of one person. The Tao Te Ching is attributed to Lao Tzu. The Hermetica is attributed to Hermes Trismegistus. In both cases, scholars believe that instead of being the work of one person, both works are more likely the result of the work of several authors contributing to a core philosophy over a period of time.

Though relatively unknown to most of us in modern society, the Hermetic writings and the philosophy they put forth so long ago have had a tremendous influence on Western thought and Western society. It would truly be impossible to over-state how much input this philosophy has had in contributing to modern thought. Every religion and philosophy we have seems to have its roots in these Hermetic teachings. There is a very long list of people who claim these Egyptian teachings to be at the core of their success. Some of these people include Leonardo da Vinci, Paracelsus, Shakespeare, Roger Bacon, Sir Isaac Newton, Sir Walter Raleigh, Daniel Defoe and Carl Jung, just to name a few.

Many Islamic philosophers claim their inspiration is due to these ancient Egyptian writings and the Jews actually equate Hermes with their prophet Enoch. The mystical Sufis of the Islamic world also trace their knowledge back to the Hermetic teachings, claiming Hermes to be the prophet Idris in their religion- the earliest teacher of recorded history who had revealed a "single doctrine" to the world. In short, some of the greatest thinkers of our time claim to have studied the Hermetic teachings, and through them, found the wisdom within them to put forth the great works they eventually produced. Many of our religious leaders and prophets of the past claim Hermes as a founder, each religion having a different name they had given him. Even the ancient teachings of India are said to be based on the teachings of Hermes. Early Greek thought was simply their interpretation of Egyptian philosophy.

The reason we do not know the extensive links between modern thought and its Egyptian and early Greek origins has to do mostly with early Christian and Muslim biases. The early Christian and Muslim churches did their best to abolish the Hermetic teachings, often with the use of torture, and worse. This in spite of the fact, as you will see soon, that both of these religions seemed to borrow extensively from the Hermetic beliefs that were so common at the time that these religions were gaining ground. As has been said so often, it is the winners who write the history books. The Hermetic influence on our lives have for the most part been left out of those history books by those that wrote them.

Another reason we in modern society are often unacquainted with the philosophy of the early Egyptians, in spite of the influence their teachings have had on us, is their belief that their teachings should never, ever be laid down into a creed of worship. They believed that they had simply uncovered the truth of this world and what lay beyond, and that this truth was beyond individual religion. The truth was for each person to see and actually experience for him or herself. Each person had to see beyond the veil for him or herself. The best any of us can do is to help the interested person find and see this truth for him or herself. This is in direct contrast to the common modern belief that only the priests of a particular religion or denomination knows the truth for sure, and that each member of that religion is required to blindly rely on that priest's guidance as to what we should believe and how we should behave.

The Egyptians knew that if their teachings were made into a definite, set creed, or even an orthodox philosophy, the main goal of their teachings would change from a personal quest for the experience of the infinite into a dogmatic set of rules. As a result, instead of leading those who were ready to the truth of this world, the teachings would instead be turned into set of orthodox religious teachings or philosophies policed by intolerant church leaders within those religions. The Egyptian belief of the necessity of an actual experience with the truth of this world would be replaced with dogmatic teachings set down in absolutes.

Further, the Egyptians knew that if their teachings were changed from an experienced-based path to one of dogmatic creeds and interpretations set down in absolutes, different religions would form, and different branches within each religion would form. Each religion and each denomination, created by people who had not actually seen the truth yet, would champion a different interpretation of the same teachings, each believing their view and only their view to be the correct one. Each group may even use the teachings to obtain money and power, and eventually would kill and die over their own interpretations of the teachings. It seems they did not underestimate the impact of religious intolerance, as we can see in our modern world, or the use of religion, and our fear of death, to make money.

Instead, the ancient Egyptians put forth the ideas and concepts that they believed may help guide us to the truth behind our existence, and encouraged us all to study those ideas for ourselves until their meanings became clear and we could pierce the veil for ourselves. Once we "pierced the veil", Life would suddenly open up to us in a completely different way. We would see beyond what we now know, into the infinite. And we would see our part in that infinite. Life would take on new meaning, the veil would be lifted (so to speak) and our lives would never be the same again. We would then be as gods among men. Not THE God, but our understanding would make us masters over our own lives to the extent that we would seem to regular people as if we were more than mere men and women. Knowing our immortality and what lay beyond would make us all but immune to the fears of this world, especially the main fear- the fear of death. We would be "born again" (note the use of this idea in modern Christian teachings), and though we still existed in this world, we would no longer believe we were of this world. We would be "reborn". We would be "awakened".

Such people that had penetrated the truth of this world, like Buddha and Christ, were simply people, just like you and me, that had pierced the veil of the world, like Hermes before them. Once awakened, like Hermes, the Buddhas and Christs of this world then did their best to help lead the rest of us past the veil, to witness "the Soul of the Universe" for ourselves. Unfortunately, the masses tended to worship the messengers and fight over the meanings of their words instead of simply trying to follow the path they were trying to lead us to. Buddha was once asked if he were a man, a god or the God. His answer was simply "I am awake".

The term "hermetic" in modern terms means "sealed", "secret", "closed tight so that nothing can escape", like a hermetically sealed container. The Egyptians felt that the true secrets of life would only be available to those who were ready to hear them. There was no need in trying to force conversion to their beliefs, like so many of the major religions have at some point in their existence. Instead, the only way to obtain the knowledge the Hermetic teachings lead to was to be ready to hear them. Once you were ready, the teachings would begin to make sense. In this way, the teachings were naturally hidden and kept safe from those who would misuse them, for those who would do such things would be unable to penetrate the mysteries. Not throwing their "pearls to the swine" is another example of a Hermetic teaching that found its way into the sayings of the modern religion of Christianity.

Like their teachings, the Hermetic followers also did not fall into creed or orthodoxy. The Hermetic followers have never sought public approval for their beliefs, or tried to form orthodox groups. The path is an independent path that most people are not ready for, and one we must all walk on our own. We can discuss ideas with each other, and help guide each other, but ultimately the "awakening" is an individual journey we all have to experience for ourselves. The truth is not a saying or a hymn, it is an experience. Most followers of this philosophy prefered to be anonymous, wanting to avoid the persecution that tends to follow having beliefs that the majority in society do not. In the past, having different beliefs could lead to torture and death. In modern society it is typically no longer quite that bad, but there is definitely still quite a bit of persecution none-the-less.

Other than the authorship, there are other similarities between the Tao Te Ching and the Hermetic philosophy of the Egyptians and Greeks. Both groups look at God as an Intelligence that is unfathomable. IT is beyond our comprehension. We can give IT names and ponder IT, but IT is beyond our grasp.

In addition, on a practical note, beyond the talk of seeing beyond the "veil" of this world into the "Soul of the Universe", both groups see human suffering in the world as we know it as a simple consequence of living against the rules of this world. Whatever IT is that we call God, IT just is. IT creates. IT does not favor one over another- IT makes the sun shine on both sinners and saints, the wealthy and the poor. IT also makes hurricanes and tornados and earthquakes, all experienced, once again, by sinners and saints alike, and by peoples of every economic condition and walk of life. There is no punishment. Life simply IS. The material world we live in has rules, rules that cannot be broken. However, the better you are at understanding the rules of life, the better you will be at harnessing Life's powers, and the better you will be at avoiding going against

Life's flow. The end result being that you will suffer less and understand more, and have an easier life. By flowing with IT, you will also come to understand IT more.

If you were to go outside naked and wet during the winter, you will most likely get sick. If you were to go out wearing very warm clothing during one hundred degree weather, again, you will be more likely to get sick. There is no favoritism, only understanding. God is not punishing you. God made this world a certain way, and you simply went against the way things work, the way your body works, and suffered the natural consequences as a result. The more you understand the rules of this life and the more you flow with the way it all works instead of against the way things work, the easier things become, the happier you will be and the less struggle and suffering you will encounter. The more you swim against the tide of life however, the more you will suffer. Suffering is not a punishment from the All-Mighty. Instead, it is simply that you violated a natural law and suffered due to conflict with natural forces. This suffering is meant to encourage you to learn, in order to hopefully avoid the same suffering in the future.

Life is simply set up a certain way, with certain rules. This is not only true on the physical realm, like the previous example of going outside naked during the winter, there are also rules and laws for the mental / emotional and spiritual aspects of life as well. The more you go against these natural laws, the more you suffer, not by way of an angry diety, but by ignorance of or defiance against the natural way of things. For this reason, Hermetic philosophy, very similar to Taoist philosophy, urges exploration. Exploring this world is every bit as spiritual as it is practical. IT created this world. Studying this world and better understanding its laws not only prevents simple suffering, such as the avoidance of discomfort and possible illness by wearing warm clothing during the winter, but by studying ITs creations, exploring is also a spiritual path. The world is a neverending mystery, and IT is the mystery behind that mystery, the Intelligence back of it all. By studying this mysterious world, you get a glimpse at the Intelligence that runs it. By studying the works of the Creator, you come to a feeling of kinship with that Creator. Think of your favorite author or actor for example. Through study and appreciation of their works, you come to have a feel and appreciation for the author of those works, even if only a little.

An interesting difference between the Taoist approach and the Hermetic approach is that the Egyptians taught that while you cannot go against the rules of life without suffering, you can use one law against the other to "seemingly" get around certain laws. *The Kybalion* goes into this idea in great detail. A very practical example would be the use of a jet engine to defy gravity. Gravity is a law we cannot break, but by using our minds we can find a way to defy gravity. The same is true on the emotional and spiritual levels as well. The main rules of life and how to use them properly is the central teaching of the Kybalion portion of the Hermetic works.

The seasons rhythmically play out in a never ending cycle. Gravity holds all the billions upon billions of heavenly bodies in place, maintaining order. The infinite atoms and orbiting electrons, so similar to our heavenly bodies, are also held in perfect order by natural laws. Our bodies, intricately complex, being maintained in amazing order, aging through cycles very similar to the cycles of the seasons, and the larger cycles of the seasons of the universe. All these things, and so many more, are all done at once, tirelessly, ceaselessly.

Studying the Universe is meant to make our lives easier, and to inspire awe and reverence. Whatever the Intelligence is behind it all, IT is beyond comprehension. There is so much to learn, so much to explore. Infinite lifetimes could not reveal all the mysteries we have waiting for us. IT is meant to be explored, the Universe is meant to be explored. The study of what IT created and still creates IS science. Reverence for IT is religion. Science and religion go together.

Children are born naturally curious. They absorb information like sponges. Adults are the same. We are happiest and most productive when we are exploring and learning. Hermetic and Taoistic philosophy and religion encourage man to do what we naturally want to do- explore, create, learn. Branch out, seek more- always. For this reason, Hermetic societies tended to flourish. Discovery and excitement over creating and exploring was the engine driving those societies to happiness and wealth, in every meaning of the word. Whenever and wherever Hermetic teachings were put forth, society seemed to flourish. Whenever the teachings were outlawed and banned, and free thought inhibited, societies tended to sink into darker times.

The famous library of Alexandria is a prime example of the open minded inspiration of the Hermetic traditions. The Alexandria library contained thousands and thousands of scrolls, putting forth ideas and teachings of a wide variety of thinkers from a wide variety of backgrounds. Learning about the wonders of the world was not just encouraged, but celebrated. Coming up with new ideas and testing out new theories was the height of man's powers, and what he was supposed to do.

Unfortunately, Hermetic teachings eventually came in direct contrast with the intolerance of the early Christian Church. The leaders of the early Christian Church saw life as set, all knowledge being contained in the Bible, or at least their version of the Bible. Chapters and entire books of the Bible that the early Christian church did not like were excluded from their Bibles. Additionally, the wisdom of the Bible was believed to be correctly interpreted only by a chosen representative who would instruct the masses on what to believe. Knowledge to them was set, and exploring on your own, or outside the Bible, was just as heretical as the apple was to Eve in Genesis.

In lieu of these beliefs, the early Christian Church burned the library of Alexandria and outlawed Hermeticism, as well as all other beliefs. One of the last great scientists and philosophers of the library of Alexandria was seized by a mob of Christians. They removed her flesh with scallop shells and then burned her body. Their leader, Bishop Cyril, was sainted.

Ironically, it has been estimated that more people have been tortured and killed over religious beliefs than in all the other wars we have had on earth, undertaken for all other reasons. The early Christian Church was a major contributer to this. Please note that the actions of the early Christian Church do not reflect, at least in my opinion, the teachings of Jesus. Many scholars have noted the difference between the teachings of Christ and the actions of His followers. Gandhi once remarked: "I like your Christ. I do not like your Christians. Your Christians are so unlike your Christ."

Whenever the Hermetic teachings come forth, we tend to experience times of progression and learning. An example of this is the Rennaissance, which was inspired by the Hermetic teachings of the Ancient Egyptians and Greeks. Whenever the Hermetic teachings have been banned or suppressed, we tend to experience bad times. An example of this, as previously mentioned, is when the early Christian Church burned the library of Alexandria and outlawed free thought. When this happened, society went into the Dark Ages. In fact, the Renaissance, meaning "rebirth", marked the end of the Dark Ages brought on by religious intolerance, and the rebirth of free thought. The Hermetic teachings were directly responsible for this Renaissance.

After the religious persecution of the early Christians, the die-hard Hermetic philosophers eventually moved on and settled largely in Arabic areas, areas now held by the Islamic states. As a result of the influence of the Hermetic philosophers, free thought and exploration in these Arabic areas blossomed and the peoples of those areas became infatuated with exploration of the world and the philosophies of Egypt and ancient Greece. As a result, these Arabian peoples are credited with a multitude of contributions to modern society. In fact, for five hundred years, the Arab world eagerly absorbed the ancient Egyptian and Greek philosophies and dominated the world. The Hermetic philosophy gave them a superior civilization, based on learning and knowledge.

Some of the Arabic contributions during this time include art and architecture, astronomy, mathematics, chemistry, physics, medicine and music.

In astronomy, the Arabian culture perfected numerous instruments used in observation still used today. They discovered irregularities in the moon's highest latitude, third lunar inequality, studied eclipses and were even able to forecast sunspots. Some of the great astronomers, like Copernicus, Kepler and Bacon stood on the shoulders of these Arabian astronomical findings.

In chemistry, the Arabs were the first to discover sulfuric acid, nitric, potassium and silver nitrate among others. They discovered the processes of distillation, crystallization and coagulation. They discovered the making of paper from cotton, linen and rags, which replaced the silk paper of the Chinese.

These Arabians had a passion for travel as well. They were the first to explore distant regions like China, Africa and Russia. They traveled and created maps. It is possible that the works of Averroes, an Arabic physician who traveled extensively, was the inspiration that led to Christopher Columbus discovering the New World. Averroes was the first to suggest the possible existence of the New World.

The Arabs discovered, invented and passed on arithmetic, geometry, algebra and trigonometry. In fact, the word Algebra is taken from the Arabic word Al Gabr. The terms "sine", "cosine" and "tangent" were first used by Al Battani, one of their most famous astronomers.

The numerals we use today are Arabic numerals. Zero was invented by bin Ahmed in 976. We didn't get the concept of zero in the West until the 13th century.

The Arabic world also contributed greatly to medicine. Books written by famous Arabic physicians contributed to the library of the Paris Faculty of Medicine in 1935. Ibn Sina, the greatest of all Arab physicians, wrote the Qanun fi-l-Tibb (the Cannon of Medicine), which is considered a master work that served as the basis for French and Italian medical exploration for over six hundred years.

The Arabs were even the first to work with Optics, and correctly gave explanations and descriptions of the eye, the lens and how vision works.

The Arabs invented mechanical clocks, the reciprocating engine and the compass (the Chinese invented the compass, the Arabs perfected it).

The Arabs even entered the realm of social sciences, improving on the current idea of governing bodies. The Arabs viewed moderate taxes as the best incentive to create a good working environment, and saw state intervention as a hinderance to the development of normal economy.

Unfortunately, Islam eventually became the main religion of the Arabic areas and over time became just as authoritarian and intolerant as the early Christian Church had been. As a result, Hermetic teachings were once again frowned upon and suppressed (usually violently), and the nation of Islam receded into darker times. The more religious extremism and intolerance we experience, the worse our lives seem to get.

A man named Giordano Bruno came to believe that the Egyptian philosophy of Hermes was the ancestor of the Greek Mystery Schools, the Jewish Religion, the Christian Religion, the Islamic Religion, and was therefore a unifying religion which all faiths could meet and resolve differences. He was arrested by the Roman Catholic Church, tortured for eight years and then burned alive.

Still, the Hermetic writings contain passages very similar to Jewish, Chrisitan, Muslim and Greek works, among others. One of the central themes of Hermetic wisdom that shows up in the Christian religion was that the "Word" of God created this world. There are so many similarities between the Hermetic teachings and our modern religions that later scholars initially believed that the Hermetic works must be more modern, copycatting quite a bit of the newer religions. We now know that this is not true- it is the other way around. All of the subsequent religions that are so prominent today seem to have borrowed liberally from Hermetic philosophy.

The influence of Hermetic teachings on early Christianity is now beyond doubt. Moses was brought up Egyptian and many early Christians lived in Egypt. In 1945, many Hermetic teachings were found amongst early Christian scriptures of the Gnostic Christians in Nag Hammadi, and there were numerous, numerous copies of these Hermetic works. All proof suggests the Heremetic writings were studied extensively by the early Christians, and incorporated into the new Christian religion. There were even caves in the Nag Hammadi area that were inhabited by hermits of the early Christian churches. The walls of these caves were littered with hieroglyphs ascribed to Hermes.

"Gnostic" means knowledge, and these early Gnostic Christians often combined the Hermetic search for knowledge into their own new religion. A central theme of the Hermetic teachings is that the goal is to "awaken" and become spiritually "reborn". The Gnostic Christians took this concept and applied the idea to Jesus Christ. Their goal was, through knowledge of Christ, to be "reborn" into Him. This is where being a "born again" Christian seems to come from, yet it is based on a Hermetic teaching. The early Christians simply borrowed the concept of being "reborn" and applied it to their own beliefs.

Hermeticists claim that the reason so many teachings in our modern religions seem contradictory is because each religion only borrowed bits and pieces of the entire Hermetic philosophy. Each religion, they believe, took only what it wanted or needed and combined the teachings with its own philosophy. As a result, many of the teachings within these newer religions seem contradictory. Studying the Hermetic philosophy is believed to unite the teachings into one unified whole, reconciling many divergent views.

One of the more central teachings of the Hermetic Philosophy is what is known as "alchemy". According to legend, alchemy is the study of chemistry and other natural sciences that allows the master to turn a base metal- something common and not valuable, like lead- into something of much higher and rarer quality- something pure, something invaluable- like gold. By burning off all that was heavy and crude in a metal, it was believed you would be left with what was pure and good- which was gold. Obviously, such knowledge would make a person rich beyond measure- they could simply turn everyday common metals into gold. Many, many people have tried to obtain such knowledge over the years.

True alchemy though is quite a bit different. The purification of something crude and worthless into something pure and priceless wasn't meant to be taken literally, materially, but is instead symbolic of something much more valuable- the purification of a crude human soul into something more intelligent, something more pure, something priceless. Knowledge shines the light on Life. Knowledge allows you to live better now, but also, certain kinds of knowledge lets you glimpse the immortality of the Mind, the immortality of the Soul. This kind of knowledge lets you get a glimpse of your higher self, and a glimpse of IT, the Intellligence behind the scenes. This kind of knowledge is transformative, and more valuable to your well-being and understanding than all the gold in the world. Once you understand the rules of this world, you navigate it better. And once you see that you are not your body, that you go on after death, what could there be to harm you? Or cause you to worry and suffer? Gold may be nice in this world, but this kind of knowledge transcends what all the gold in the world could ever bring us.

The goal of Hermetic Wisdom is to pass along this knowledge, both of the rules of this world so that you may live better here and now, but also of what is beyond this world, and what you are beyond this world. Then you would be free. Free in this life. Free of the fear of death. Free of everything. You are consciousness itself, unbound, unfettered... completely free. You may seem to be this body, but once you see that you are simply consciousness stuck in the body for a short time, everything changes.

Hermes Trismegistus is credited with being the founder of the Hermetic philosophies. He lived in the days of "old Egypt", when the current races of men were considered to be in infancy. His influence was so strong that he eventually became linked with the Egyptian god Thoth and the Greek god Hermes. In fact, the Egpytian legend is that his knowledge transformed him into a god. Not THE God, but as a god here on earth. His last name Trismegistus actually means "thrice great"- kind of like saying he is not just great, not just great great, but three times as great as any greatness you have ever known or can imagine. He lived before Jesus, possibly before Moses, and is believed to have been a contemporary of Abraham. Some even claim he was Abraham's teacher. Others believe he may have actually been Moses. During the Renaissance, Hermes was linked with Moses and believed to be the founding father of Judeao-Christian beliefs. He was considered a central figure in the Rennaissance's vision of a philosophy that united Religion and Science. Who knows? All of this is unfortunately lost to history.

Like so many other philosophical and religious founders and leaders, Hermes is said to have received his knowledge in a vision during a period of deep concentration. Jesus, after being baptized by John the Baptist, went out into the Judaean Desert for forty days and forty nights, fasting and meditating. Buddha, similarly, meditated and fasted for forty five days and nights under a Bodhi tree. Muhammad of the Islamic religion received his visions after meditating alone in a cave. Even Socrates is said to have received his knowledge from a divine vision he had after a very long period of concentration and contemplation. This is a very common scenario among the leaders and founders of different religions and philosophies. During Hermes' awakening, God is said to have revealed to him the truth of the world, how it works, and what lies beyond. Hermes is said to have seen "the Soul of the Universe".

The Hermetica is Hermes' attempt to describe, to the best of his ability, what is ultimately indescribable. It is his attempt to pass on what he saw in those visions. Each chapter of *The Hermetica* describes a different aspect of what he had seen, from the meaning of time to the substance of God to the meaning of human life and why we are here. The *Hermetica* we have access to was written mostly by the Greeks. It is the Greek attempt to put into writing the teachings of ancient Egypt that had been passed down to them.

The Emerald Table, also known as the Smaragdine Tablet, is an ancient artifact purportedly molded out of a single piece of green crystal. On the tablet is written fourteen cryptic sentences that is said to sum up the secret to Alchemy and Hermetic teachings. This is similar to the tablets of Moses from the Old Testament which were believed to sum up the main rules of the Jewish religion at that time.

According to the legend surrounding *The Emerald Tablet*, a man named Balinas discovered the tablet in a vault below the statue of Hermes, who is credited with being the author of the tablet.

Inside the vault was an old corpse, possibly Hermes, on a golden throne. In the hands of the corpse was held the Emerald

Tablet. There are other variations to this story, but this is the general gist of the tablet's legendary discovery.

Translations of the fourteen statements from different authorities can be found all over the internet with a simple search. The statements are written in an arcane language and can be very hard to grasp. I believe the statements to be symbolic, and have written my own interpretation of *The Emerald Tablet* if you are interested. My version is called "The Emerald Tablet 101".

The Kybalion was originally published in 1912 by "the Three Initiates" who chose to remain anonymous. No one really knows who these people are, though they claim to be carriers of the torch of Hermes' teachings, which have been handed down from Master to student for thousands of years. The authors of *The Kybalion* claim the book to be a clarification of an ancient, unpublished work that had only been seen by initiates into the system. In other words, whereas *The Hermetica* is supposed to represent Hermes' vision and subsequent teachings, *The Kybalion* is supposed to represent inner teachings based on *The Hermetica* as handed down internally from Hermetic teacher to Hermetic student over thousands of years. Some authorities do not feel this to be true, that the Kybalion is instead a more modern interpretation of Hermetic wisdom mixed with new age philosophies. In any event, *The Kybalion* gets more specific on the exact working of the "Laws of Life" and how to apply them successfully.

As with the Tao Te Ching and many other thought systems, the Hermeticists do not aggressively push their teachings and beliefs. So many religions push conversion to their ways and beliefs through aggressive persuasion. Sometimes that persuasion is simply verbal, sometimes political, sometimes it is through social pressuring and sometimes it has been at the point of a blade, or by torture. The Hermeticists do not work in this manner at all. They do not push or try to persuade. It is against their beliefs. They believe the truth exists, and that it is ready to be discovered by anyone who wants to find it. When the student is ready, the teachings will find their way to them. Until then, even if a person were to discover these teachings, if the person was not ready for them, then the individual would find no meaning in the teachings.

What follows is my interpretation of the Hermetic teachings. As with my book on the Tao Te Ching, what I am really after is expressing the Big Picture. I believe we very often get so caught up in the minute details of a philosophy or religious teaching that we miss the big picture.

I also try to interpret the Hermetic teachings in a way that is more easily understood in our modern times. Some of what the Hermetic teachings taught is in a language very hard to interpret into modern society. It is not just that they used a different language than ours, it is also that the writers of that day often used examples or parables to get their points across that people in modern day life would have no reference to. For example, thousands of years from now someone reading works from this current era may have no idea what a cell phone is, what internet explorer is, or what a BFF is. If we used those things in our teachings, future generations would have no idea what we were talking about.

Much of the Hermetic writings we have are not original works, but interpretations by the Greeks, who were trying to explain the ancient Egyptian philosophy to their generation. I am trying to do the same- interpreting the ancient Egyptian works in an easy to understand format for our day and age. In that vein, I used some modern language that was not in the original to point out the similarities in thought between the ancient Egyptians and some of our own teachings. The use of the words Ki and Qi, the Garden of Eden, etc were my doing. The phrase "Word of God" though is very much Hermetic.

I'd like to make one last point. In some of the oldest religions and philosophies (for example, the Sutras of the Hindu religion), it has been pointed out that there are many different major teachings, all of which lead to the same goal. All paths, according to these teachings, are equally valid. They all lead to God, whatever God may be, but take different paths. The benefit of different paths is that each person is different. The path one person takes may not make sense to the next person. Your best path depends on individual inclination. All paths are needed so that each person can find the path that works best for him or her. Most people have a dominant path that they have an affinity for, but there may also be mixtures of paths that work best for them.

The main paths include (1) service to others, (2) knowledge, learning, wisdom, (3) mental stillness, deep concentration as in meditation and (4) faith and devotion to God. All four of these paths, or mixtures, are believed to be paths to God. You simply have to find the way you most prefer, what comes most natural to you.

Some also believe that though you have one or two main paths that make the most sense to you, that as you progress, all four end up becoming more and more a part of you. For example, through knowledge you might obtain an inner stillness as you come to understand IT more. You may study the Universe and come to understand the Intelligence that created and runs it. Along with that, you may become more and more interested in helping others. Eventually you feel ITs presence more and more, and your belief and therefore faith grow as well. In this way, though one or two paths may be your main route, in the end you often end up displaying evidence of all the paths in your life.

The Hermetica and especially the Kybalion seems to be aimed more towards the Path of Knowledge as the launching point, though as you will see, deep concentration is also a major part.

HERMES' INTRODUCTION

There are reasons that I, Hermes
Am laying down on paper
My experiences
With the Infinite

First, is to help guide others
To experience the Soul of the World
As I have been so lucky
To experience myself

Secondly,
I live in a spiritual era
Where science and religion
Come together

It will not always be so

Soon science and religion
Will separate

Some will choose science

Others, religion
But neither will see
That they are one
And the same

Religion is the study of God
Science is the study of what God created

Through study
Of the natural world
You come to appreciate
The perfect order of the Universe
And you are overcome with awe
And reverence

And you should be

The Universe is a marvel
And every part of it a marvel,
All working perfectly
Precisely
Nothing out of place
Or mistaken
Even for a second

Not one piece of it
Misplaced

From atoms to planets
From electrons to solar systems
All things are in their place

And perfect
And perfectly ordered-
Every square inch

When this split
Between science and religion occurs
The experience I had
Will become more needed
Than ever
For people will have ceased to see the miracle
Of this world

They will have lost their sense of wonder
And reverence
For the miracle
Of Life

Man will grow weary of living
Having lost
The mystery of it all

Dark times will ensue,
For religion without science
Is ignorant, and intolerant
While science without religion
Is lonely, and smug

What I experienced
Is not a clever philosophy
Based on arguments and opinions
But instead a reality

That transcends opinion
Once experienced directly

So I write
For that future generation
When religions bicker
Over trivial matters
And science thinks
It has surpassed even God

I write for that time
When man is lonely
Because he has lost the miracle
And has become weary
Of Life

CHAPTER ONE

Once
When I was deep in silence
And my mind was focused
In deep concentration
And I was wholly intent
In my focus
I experienced
Something dramatic,
Something beyond my normal perception
And understanding

My senses seemed to suspend
As if withdrawn during sleep
And I traveled beyond my thoughts

My mind was alert
And clear
And my understanding
Surpassed
Any clarity
I had ever known

In this state
It seemed
A vast and boundless Intelligence
Emerged into my mind's eye

This Intelligence seemed to know me
And called me by name

"What are you looking for, Hermes?"
IT seemed to say
Yet I heard without my ears
And saw without my eyes
I experienced IT with my mind
Or my heart

"Who are you?" I asked

"I am God.
I am Consciousness ITself.
I am Atum,
As your kind calls me."

"I created you and am part of you,
And am with you always
And everywhere.

"I know what you seek"
IT seemed to say without speaking
And I heard, and understood
"But hold in your mind all you want to know
And I will show you…"

"I seek the nature of Reality." I answered
"I want to pierce the veil of this world
And to see beyond,
I want to know
What Life
Is all about

"I want find God
I long to meet
The Soul of the Universe
Please show me!" I begged
"I have to know!
I have to see!"

Suddenly everything shifted before me
And Reality opened into view

It was as if in a dream
But much clearer
Yet beyond comprehension

Something I understood
Not by logic
But by something deeper within

It was an experience
Truly beyond the intellect
Of us all,
Even the wisest
Who have ever lived

The experience
Was beyond understanding
Impossible to put to words
Or logic
But I will try
To give a rough estimate
Of what I saw
Or more precisely
What I felt
Or somehow knew

I saw boundless Light
I saw IT within me
Felt IT within me
And IT was infinite

The Light was infinite
There was no end to it
In any direction

The Light was all there was
And all that could be

The Light was Consciousness
IT was Intelligence
IT was Science
And IT was Religion

The Light was gentle, joyous
And I was filled
With such a longing for IT

When I saw IT
That I can't even put into words
The depth
Of my longing-
Like coming home
After years of being away

The Light was Love
As if Love were a physical substance
And the actual substance
Of the Universe

And it *was*
Love *was* the substance
Of the Universe
And it *was*
The underlying essence
Of all that was

Not jealous love
Or puppy love
Or lustful love
Or cheap or silly love
But something deeper
Something much more substantial

And then I saw Creation
I saw the Universe being born
It happened before me
Yet within me

Out of the Oneness
Out of the One
Out of the Light
Was birthed a shadow
Darker and heavier
Than the Light

The darkness was separated from the Light
And birthed
As if in a great explosion
Of Light and Energy

The darkness exploded
And stretched out
In all directions
And like all births
It seemed painful
And violent

Compared to the Light
The dark seemed lonely
And scary
And heavy

At first the dark was chaotic,
A tangled mess
Expanding from the explosion,
Swirling without order

But then a Word or a Thought
Or an Idea

Seemed to emerge from the Light
And it entered the dark womb
Of matter

IT seemed a vibration
That entered the creation
And the chaotic substance
Of the darkness calmed
And slowly cooled
Into the body of the world
We know

And at the same time
Order began to ensue
And motion…
Continuous motion
Precise

The Light then asked me
"Do you understand what you have seen?
For such things are as of yet beyond
Your abilities to comprehend."

"I am the Light" IT went on
"Which existed before Creation-
The Light of Consciousness

"I am that Consciousness
I am Consciousness Itself.

"You are Consciousness as well

But on a lesser scale
And embedded in physical form
For now

"You are not your body
You are , as I AM
The Consciousness within

"That which sees and hears within you
That is you
Not the physical form of your body
Nor the thoughts that rise and fall

"The Watcher within you-
That is you

"What you saw
In your inner vision
Was the One
Which is Me

"Before Creation
I existed
Without a beginning
Without an end
For time is a worldly concept
And has no place in Consciousness

"Out of Me
Out of a thought
I created your Universe

And everything in It

"Using part of myself
To create
And to imbue all that exists
With substance
And Soul
And therefore Life
And motion

"I birthed Life
And the material world
Which you saw as a darkness
From Myself
Through my will to create

"I then thought order into my creation-
I imagined it,
I willed it
And continue to do so

"In the beginning
There was only the One
And there was neither
Male nor female
For I am neither male
Nor female

"Yet with My word
With my will
Your Universe was split into two

The male and the female
The positive and the negative

"The dynamic
Between these two poles
Keeps all Life in motion
Like a battery
Or generator
Of all Life
As you know it

"Due to this polarity
All things went into motion
From atoms to stars
From solar systems to entire Universes
And they stay in motion
As is My desire

"Due to the polarity
Of male and female
In living beings
They too
Have gone forth and multiplied
And continue to do so
As is My desire

"This world is teeming with Life
Again, as is My desire

"The order
I put order into this world-

You call It Nature

"Her laws are immutable
Nature is Nature
She just is
And her laws are what they are

"Your body is of Nature
So you are prisoner
To Her laws

"As long as you have a body
You have Nature's Laws
Governing it

"But your Mind is not
A prisoner to the body
Or the world you know-
Your body is subject to the Laws of Nature
But your Mind is free

"Your Consciousnes
Like Mine
Is unbound, unfettered
Uncontainable

"Your Mind
Can take you to Heaven or Hell
Create a better Life
Or a worse Life
For it creates what it wills

For better or worse

"With your mind
You can course the stars
And explore other worlds,
All without leaving the Earth
And even more can it do
As you will see
At some point

"We are creators
You and I

"I made you in my image
In My likeness,
Not your body…
Your Conciousness
I *am* Consciousness
And you *have* Conciousness

"Consciousness *is*
The miracle you seek

"You are as My child
And I love you
As My child

"And just as your Mind
Produces thoughts
And gives birth
To creations

So too does Mine
Yet on a grander scale

"When you saw my Creation
You wanted to create as well
And add to my creation
And explore
And I allowed it

"So you descended into form
To create
And add to my works,
And to explore

"Of all the living things on earth
Man alone is double-
Mortal, because you have a body
Bound by the laws of this world
But immortal
Because of the real You within,
Conciousness Itself
Unbound and free

"The lower animals have Conciousness
But not to this scale-
They cannot travel
With their minds
Or create
As you and I can

"No other living creature

Has your level of consciousness

"This is the miracle!

"That man is unique
A mix of nature
And immortal Consciousness
A slave to Nature
Until the world of Nature
Is left behind

"Man received his body
From the heavy darkness,
The world of matter
But man received his Consciousness
His Mind
From his Father

"So I created this world
And I made it pregnant with Life
And form
And movement
And allowed you
To contribute as well

"All that is
I did
With a word, an idea
An intent

"There is nothing dead

In this world
Not a thing without soul
For I am the Consciousness
Of Life
The Intelligence behind matter,
Behind *all* matter
I am what makes it all alive

"I am the Soul you seek
I am the Soul of the Universe

"I am Light and Life
I am physics and biology
I am astronomy and astrophysics
I am the Intelligence
That runs this world

"I am that which
You and your kind call God
With many different names
Killing and torturing each other
Over the different names
You each prefer

"I am that which scientists call Nature
And gravity and cohesion
Algebra and trigonometry
And so many other things

"I am Creation Itself
I am the Big Bang

The original Creator
And I am evolution as well

"Every atom
Every electron
Every quasar
Every solar system
Every dimension
Every cell and organ of the body-
All these things and more
I created, breathed life into
And animate
To this very day

"And I am the Intelligence
That alters the bodies and minds of organisms
Over generations
In response to their dealings with life
As they better adapt
To their surroundings

"I do that as well-
What you call evolution

"Do you understand?"

I am not sure
That I did understand
Not all of it anyway
In fact, I am sure that I did not

But what I did grasp
What I was able to absorb...
The feelings it left me with...
There are no words
To describe

I was filled with a joy
I had never known
And a longing
For that Light

I was so overcome
So in love with that Light

But then a fear came over me
For I so longed for the Light
That all my other earthly desires
Had become foolish
Compared to my longing
For the Light

I feared losing this vision,
This knowledge

I feared it would fade
I feared this
More than anything
I had ever feared before

"Please!" I begged
"No matter what else happens

Please don't ever let me forget
what you have shown me here!!"

"The choice is yours"
the Light seemed to say.
"To remember. And to walk the path.
Or not to."

"How do I stay with the knowledge?"
I begged.
"How do I remain
In the light?"

"The most important thing
Is to remember
What you have just seen

"You are not of this world
You are of the Light

"This world is your garment
For now
Not your home

"It is normal
To need things
In this world

"You need clothing
You need money
You need friends

You need food

"It is also normal
To have an ego
And to have thoughts

"Your ego
Is there to protect you
Without it
You would not last long
On this earth

"Your mind is a tool as well
Designed to suggest information
To you
To give you ideas
As to how the situation before you
Has been handled in the past
And how you may handle it now

"Your thoughts are a mixture
Of your personality
And your experiences
But they are not you

"They are meant to be
A tool for your use
Not your master

"Using the things
Of this world…

Your ego, your thoughts
And material things
Are normal
And needed
But attachment to these things
Are not

"Realize that you are not your body
Or your thoughts
Or your ego
But the Consciousness within

"That is what sets you free

"In addition
Remember that Light
Is attracted to Light

"To attract the Light
Act like the Light
Be like the Light
And immediately
You are in the Light

"The Light is giving
So give
The Light is compassionate
So be compassionate
The Light is creative
So create
The Light is not arrogant

So how can you be?

"The Light gives
Without the thought of receiving
Or reward
And the Light loves
Unconditionally

"I am Love
To know me,
Love

"Can you do this?
If so, you will be
In the Light
And you will feel it
And know it

"You will not feel
The full Light
Until you shed
That body
But you can feel
ITs presence
Here and now nonetheless

"The Light makes you happy
You know when you are in IT

"Conversely
Not being in the Light

Is scary
And dark

"You either choose the Light
Or you choose the dark

"Each moment
If you realize from whence you come
And you do good
You feel the Light

"But when you become attached
To material things
You become obsessed
And selfish

"You can never get enough-
You will always need more
For it is the Light you seek
It is the Light you all seek

"But you often become lost in the dark
While looking for for the Light

"You mistake the joy
Of the temporary desires on earth
For the real Treasure
You all long for

"Attachment, jealousy
Acting selfishly

Harming others
Doing bad deeds
Stealing
These are all dark deeds

"They are not of the Light
They are of the dark
And darkness does not mix well
With the Light
As oil does not mix well
With water

"They separate
And exist alone

"When you choose the heavy darkness
You feel it
And suffer
For you exist in dark
Which separates
From the Light

"A man that kills
Is not a happy man,
A man that steals
Is not a happy man,
No matter what these people do to another
No matter how bad they make another feel
They themselves suffer worse

"This is why they do what they do

They are so unhappy themselves
And seek relief from the pain
They seek the joy of the Light
But are led astray
By the temporary promises
Of the dark

"They seek the Light
But have been tempted by the dark
Whose rewards look easier to obtain
And more immediately satisfying

"But it is an illusion
And once trapped within
It is hard to get out

"The darkness breeds more darkness
Obsession breeds more obsession
The worse you feel
The more you choose the dark
The quicker you want redemption
And the worse things get,
Making you feel even worse
Causing worse behavior

"What was once enough
No longer is
And you need more
And bigger and better

"It is a vicious cycle

"When you act this way
You have separated yourself
From the Light
And you feel it

"It makes you scared
And lonely
And angry
And your bad behavior continues
And gets worse
For you are lost
From the Light
Which you seek

"You are of the Light
You crave the Light
You are meant for the Light

"When you walk away from the Light
It is no punishment of Mine,
You are choosing the darkness
Over the Light
Though you don't see this
Because you have forgotten
From whence you come"

This frightened me
More than I can say

"If a person loses his way" I said
"for years and years,

how does he get back?"

"The second he acts like the Light"
IT answered
"Or remembers the Light
He is back
No matter how long
He wandered in darkness
For the second you choose the Light
You are in the Light

"Ultimately
You all return to the Light…
Eventually,
Though you may wander
For long periods
In the dark

"The Light is a path
You choose each moment

"Over time
Once you have spent enough time
Within the Light
You become so used to IT
And feel so miserable without IT
That you will get to the point
That you will never leave IT again

"Do your best
To understand that you are immortal

That you are the Watcher within
That you are your Consciousness
And that desire, attachment
To the things of this fleeting World
Is the cause of suffering

"Attachment clouds the Watcher within
Separating you
From your own Self
And you live from your desires
Instead of from your Center

"Also learn to pity
Those in the darkness
For though they injure you
They are simply lost
And scared
And feel tortured
At the absence
Of the Light"

Thus the vision ended
As far as I can remember

Since that time
Since the time of my vision
I have come to realize
That I am now the same man I was
In so many ways

Yet at the same time

I am also vastly different-
Not even a shadow
Of my former self

I still go about my daily activities
And still need food
And still need water
And still need the things of this world
But at the same time
Knowing the Truth
Has freed me from this World
As I once knew It

I may still be *in* this World
But I am no longer *of* this World

And I will never go back

CHAPTER TWO

How do you explain IT
To someone who has not experienced IT?
How do you even begin to describe IT?

How do you put into words
So that others can understand
Or comprehend
An Entity
That is beyond words-
An entity that is beyond comprehension?

IT, Whatever IT is
Is beyond this dimension
Yet IT is the Essence
Of this dimension

IT is formless
And thoughtless
And actionless
Yet the root of all forms
And thoughts

And actions

How can this be?

IT is God
Yet any concept of IT
Falls short

IT is Science
The Intelligence behind reality
Yet we have only scratched the surface
Of the Science of this world

IT created the Universe
Yet IT is the Universe
Beyond this dimension
Unbounded by dimension
Yet IT is dimension as well
Every one of them
And there are too many to mention

IT is the God of all religions
The thought process of all philosophies
The Natural Laws studied by scientists
Yet not one religion, scientist or philosopher
Has fully comprehended

IT is beyond us
Beyond any concept we could create

Any concept or creed

Implies boundary
"IT is this"
Means there are things
IT is not
Which is not so

There simply are no limits to IT
Whatever IT is

We have all given IT names
Like God and Allah and Atum
But IT is beyond names

Even a name tries to define IT
Which cannot be done

If you want to give IT a name
You would have to call IT by all names
For IT is everything

We have no words for what IT is
Nor concepts that come close

We even try to give IT agendas
Telling others what IT wants and needs from us-
But IT is beyond our agendas
ITs intelligence and reasoning exceeds our grasp

It is as if IT is simply Consciousness Itself
Whatever that may be

As if IT is a great big Mind
And Mind alone
That created everything we know
And all the worlds and dimensions
We don't yet know

This is the closest
I think I can come to describing IT-
As a Supreme Mind
A Supreme Intelligence,
A Consciousness-
The Light of Awareness
That makes Life and Thought
And Consciousness ITself possible

What is life without Consciousness
If there were no Consciousness
There would be no awareness-
It would be as if life
Simply wasn't happening
As far as we'd be concerned

There'd be no experience

Think of your own Mind-
Think of how unbound it is
It can escape your body at any time
And roam the earth
Or the universe

With a thought

You can be with a loved one
Or at the beach
Or on Mars
Or even with a deceased friend

This imagination,
This power of the mind
That allows us to explore and marvel
And allows us to create-
This seems to be what God is,
Only we are on a much smaller scale

This is why IT is unbound
Whatever IT is
And how IT can be free and eternal
And in all places at all times

For IT *is* Mind
IT *is* Consciousness and Awareness
And imagination,
Just like we are

But we have a body
And think we are that body
While IT is has all bodies
And knows what IT really is

Just as we
Were developed for this world
In the womb,
So too

Are we being developed
For the next world
Within these bodies

Just as we emerged
From the world
Of our mother's womb
Into this world,
So too
Will we emerge
From the world of these bodies
Into the next

We are made in ITs image-
Not our bodies
But our Minds,
Our Imaginations

IT imagines and creates constantly
Continuously

IT did not create the World
And then move on

IT is active even now
At this second
Every second

IT is the ONE
The Unifying factor of Life
The Intelligence beyond and behind all that is

IT is like the number one
No matter how many times the number one
Is multiplied or divided
IT is still the number one,
Untouched
And the root of all other numbers

Just as you are one entity
That can walk and talk
Eat and breathe
Digest your food and multiply in your head
All at the same time,
So too is IT one Entity
That animates the entire Universe
All at once
As if the Universe was ITs body

All that exists
Emanates from the Imagination
Of Consciousness Itself,
The Intelligence behind it all-
The rules of Nature behind the cohesion of atoms
And the swirl of galaxies

We have said IT creates with ITs Word
But it is more like a Vibration
Emanating from a thought

This vibration we have called the Son of God
But it is more like the Thoughts of God

IT, like us
Loves to imagine and create
And explore

This is the reason we exist
And the reason IT exists-
To imagine and to create
And to explore and to play as well
Though on much different scales

In the end
We must come to realize
That our individual minds
Are fundamentally no different
Than the Great Mind
Inside which
We all live and move
And have our being

It is possible to free our minds
From the constraints of this world
And to see beyond the veil
By coming to understand
The power of our own minds
And using this knowledge
To comprehend the power
Of ITs unlimited Mind
For both minds are of the same nature
But far different degrees

When the veil of the world pulls back

You will awaken
And be reborn into the same world
You know right now

Yet this world
Though the same to others
Will then be far different for you
From the world as you know it now
For you will be free from it-
In it, but not of it

What you once saw
As the reality of this world
Becomes as a shadow
Emanating from the Great Mind
Which seems hidden
Beyond the veil

CHAPTER THREE

To know ITs being
Concentrate deeply on IT in thought

To see IT with your physical eyes
Simply become aware
Of the exquisite order
Of the Universe

Allow me to explain...

ITs essence is Mind-
Intelligence, Awareness
Consciousness

Can you physically see Mind?
No

Can you physically see Consciousness or Awareness?
Can you physically see Intelligence?
No, not with your physical eyes
But you can sense these things
With your inner vision

You can "see" ITs essence
With your Mind
With your Consciousness
With your Awareness

In order to do so
You must withdraw into yourself
And make idle the senses of the body

You must concentrate and contemplate so deeply
That the whole of this world fades away
Including your thoughts
Including your senses

Will that you may pierce the veil
And eventually
You will

By properly directing your Mind
You may eventually experience
The Great Mind

On the other hand
If you wish to see IT with your physical eyes
(Though this is not literally possible
For ITs essence is Mind
Which cannot be seen)
You can come to know IT
Through the observation of ITs works
In this world

How?

Look around you,
Look at the uncanny order of the Universe-
The precision
The vastness
The immensity

Look at the precise route of the stars,
Routes that are repeated over and over and over
Without fail

Look at the unending seasons on earth,
Also repeated over and over and over
Reliably, without fail

Look at the exact structure of atoms
And the coherent order of solar systems and galaxies

Look at the Intelligence
Of the smallest, simplest organisms that exist
Which somehow know how to move
And eat and stay alive
And reproduce

The Intelligence in that simplest organism
Is well beyond the skills
Of the greatest minds alive
To reproduce

Can the best scientist alive create

Even one amoeba from scratch?
A single bacteria?
A single fly?
Not even close

Look at yourself and ponder the vast greatness of you-
For what Intelligence must it have taken
For a sperm from your dad and an egg from your mom
To merge into one
And miraculously become a new and separate life form
Complete with Awareness,
Whatever that is,
And its own identity?

Billions of people have come and gone over the course of
time
Yet not one has been exactly like you

Look at the precision with which
You grew as an embryo

Each stage of development
Progressed along an orderly route
Predictably, dependably

Your eyes developed at a certain, known stage
Your lungs developed at another
Your heart started beating at a predictable time period
Your ears and skin developed at another

Orderly

Organized
Precise
Intelligent
Coherent

Scientists and doctors can plot
The growth of an embryo
From beginning to birth
By the schedule each embryo
Tends to keep
As it develops

The Universe is orderly beyond chance
And IT, whatever IT is
Is the Intelligence
Directing that order

Whatever you prefer to call IT-
God, Mother Nature, Science
It makes no difference

Look at how special you are
You have eyes and ears and a nose
Special senses that are beyond the greatest scientist's skill
To recreate or even reproduce

Is there a camera whose lens
Comes close to the human eye?
With living tissue that regenerates?
Wets itself, modulates itself?
Defends itself, heals itself?

And that is just one example
There are endless examples in your body-
Hearing apparatus, smelling apparatus
Apparatus for the sense of touch
Apparatus for the sense of balance
The list is unending

You have so many different
And specialized systems within you as well-
The brain and nervous system
The cardiovascular system
The digestive system
The endocrine system
And many more

These systems all work together,
They all come together as a united whole-
Each system, each tissue and each cell
Working tirelessly, intelligently, synchronistically,
systematically
With the unified objective
Of benefiting the overall organism,
Protecting it from harm
And providing it with what it needs to exist

You have arms and legs,
A skeleton to hold everything up
And muscles to make you mobile

Each body part
Is made up of living, breathing cells and tissues

Each cell is intelligent beyond belief

Each tissue is like an army of cells
Working selflessly together as a tissue

The cells create tissues
The tissues create organs
The organs create systems
And the systems come together
To create the organism

Each part along the way
Is intelligent in and of itself,
And each part is also intelligent in its overall role
Of creating and maintaining the organism

Each cell, each tissue, each organ and each system
Knows what to do
How to do it
And when
All without conscious help from you

Every part is self regulating
As is the whole

There is an immune system to defend the body
A digestive system to feed the body
An excretory system to get rid of wastes
The list of abilities of your body
Goes on without end

But the greatest miracle of all
The miracle of miracles
The pinnacle of greatness
Is that you have Consciousness

You are conscious
And you are aware
Whatever in the world that is-
Can the concept even be grasped?

And you have identity

Can science do this?
Can science create Consciousness?
Can science create Awareness?
Much less self-awareness?
Not even close

Even if science could come close
To creating a single human being from scratch
It would take hundreds
If not thousands of specialists
To put the human together

One specialist would be needed for your eyes
Another for your nose
One for your skin
Another for your lungs
One for your nervous system
Another for your endocrine glands
And so on

Yet IT
Whatever IT is
Creates a human being effortlessly
Perfectly
And not just one at a time
But countless at a time,
Each one different
Each one special and unique

This Intelligence
Not only created every person
That has ever existed
But IT also created
Every living thing
That has ever existed as well-
Bacteria and viruses
Dinosaurs and fleas
Moths and wildflowers

But that's not all
This Intelligence
Not only created
Every living thing
That has ever existed,
IT also created
Every single thing
That that has ever existed
Whether we see life in it or not-
Planets and moons
 Stars and suns
Quasars, supernovas and celestial gasses

And all the while
Simultaneously
This Intelligence was also running
The rest of the universe-
Not one star route out of place
Not a single atom
Spinning out of control

We couldn't do even one of these things
Yet this Intelligence does them all-
Effortlessly
Tirelessly
Ceaselessly

This Intelligence didn't just create us all
And then abandon us,
IT created and now maintains us

IT birthed us all, people and solar systems alike
IT made us grow, maintains us
And will eventually cause our decline
Our death
And our renewal,
As IT does with every other thing
In the Universe

All things have seasons of life don't they?
People, the earth
Solar systems, galaxies
Suns

All things go through the same seasons
Of birth and growth
Decline and death
And rebirth...
A Spring, a Summer, a Fall and a Winter
And then a Spring again

As things are on the smaller scale
So they are on the larger scale

As an atom is a small sun
Surrounded by electrons
So too is our solar system a large atom
Composed of a sun
That is surrounded by planets

As a person goes through the cycles of life
So does our planet and every other planet-
As does each solar system
Each galaxy and the Universe Itself

Could all of this be an accident?
Could all this order have happened by chance?
Just good fortune? A fluke?
A favorable coincidence
That is repeated every second
Of every minute
Of every hour
Of every day?

Only disorder is an accident,

Not order

It is true and undeniable
That Intelligence as a thing
Is invisible
But once we understand the magnificence of Life,
The miracle surrounding us,
Then we see Intelligence everywhere-
We see design

The Universe is as the body
Of this Intelligence
And we can come to know IT
By contemplating
ITs extraordinary beauty and order

Intelligence is manifest in every single thing-
ITs signature is weaved permanently
Into the very fabric of reality

If you understand these things
You cannot help but develop
An awe for this World
And through that awe
You will gain at least a grain of insight
For the Intelligence
That created it

That grain is enough

Some may say

That it is simply Nature
That created this world
And now maintains it

This is the scientist's argument

I don't disagree
For this Intelligence *is* Nature,
This Intelligence *is* the laws of Nature-
We are speaking of the same Thing

Why don't all the stars
Just fly around randomly?
Why do the planets line up correctly?
Why are the seasons so reliable?
How are the atoms able
To coherently, correctly and consistently
Form into the building blocks
Of our world?

Call this Intelligence God if you want
Or Science
Or Nature-
Whatever you desire call IT,
IT is beyond all of of these concepts

To see ITs essence
You must use your mind
But to see ITs presence in this World
You must simply recognize the marvel
That is this World

If you want to truly understand
The One unifying Force
Binding reality together
You must return to how you were as a child,
Filled with awe
By the deep mystery surrounding us
At all times and in all directions
Forever

A mystery
Whose boundaries
We have not even begun to approach

The world pulsates with Life
It is pregnant with Consciousness
All due to an Intelligence
That we cannot understand

Hidden, yet manifest through what IT creates
And what IT does

The Universe is a living work of art
Immense, vast, unending
Alive!
Created by an anonymous Force
That we cannot fathom
Hiding just beyond the curtain
Of this world

You no longer see IT
For you have lost the wonder

And take the miracle for granted

Amazement should be your constant disposition
If it is not
Then you simply don't understand
The miracle of it all

Look with your mind
And suddenly Intelligence is everywhere
IT becomes everything we see and touch

For this Intelligence
Is the Author of the Universe
And IT is beyond the Universe
And IT *is* the Universe

If you awaken
All of what I have said
Will become evident and obvious

Until then
It must be explained

CHAPTER FOUR

In the timeless beginning
There was only the One
Complete and perfect
Within ITself

There was nothing IT did not have
Nothing IT lacked
So there was nothing IT needed

IT simply was

IT was (and is) completely at peace
But IT wanted to experience-
IT wanted to create
And to explore

Being All, Unified, Whole
There was nothing to experience
For to experience, there must be something outside of
yourself
Yet there was nothing outside of IT

So IT,
Whatever IT is
Created from ITself another
So that IT may experience
And create
And explore

If IT
Had never done this
IT would only know peace
There would be nothing more to experience

If there was nothing other
Than the Garden of Eden
So to speak
A place of perfection and peace
There would never be
Any other experience

To experience joy
There must be sadness
To experience elation
There must also be sorrow and despair

In order to experience anything at all
There must be opposites
There must be duality-
There cannot only be One
There must at least be Two

So from the One came a Second-

The Son if you will
Created in ITs image
But of lower vibrational frequency

And the Son was One as well
And Whole

This Second entity, the Son
Is our World
The Cosmos, the Universe
Created out of
The Mind of God

Within this World
The One became Two-
A male and a female part,
A positive and a negative pole,
The yang and the yin,
The proton and the electron,
An alpha particle and an omega particle,
Representing the extreme range
From the most positively charged
And therefore most masculine particle
To the most negatively charged
And therefore most feminine particle

From this split
Came the union and repulsion
Of the male and the female energies and forms
Causing the Universe to divide and multiply
And to reproduced unendingly

The constant attraction and repulsion
Between the male and the female energies
Between the positive and the negative charges
Generated a Life Force
That began to animate the Universe
(And still does)

IT is this Life Force
That enlivens our bodies
Giving us Life
Every part, every cell and tissue and organ

As a battery
With its positive and negative poles
Produces energy
So too does this Great Battery
Produce Energy-
The Energy of Life,
The Life Force
That runs this World
And everything within it

The swirl of the negative electrons
Around the nucleus of an atom
Is the basic battery of Life
Producing Energy unending

The same with the suns
And the planets whirling around them

The atom is not just

The basic building block of Energy
But also
The basic building block
Of the physical forms in this World
As well

Solar systems, being large atoms
Create larger blocks of matter

Future generations
Will call this Life Force,
This Energy,
Many things-
Ki and Qi
Prana and Mana
But like the Great Intelligence
That created the Generator
There are no words
That approach what this Energy
Really is,
What IT means or what IT does

Some even call it
The Holy Spirit

The swirl of Energy
Created from the two opposing poles
At first was chaotic-
There was no order to the Cosmos,
There was no order to Life

So the Light commanded order-
IT simply thought, or willed
Order into this world
And so it was

This thought or will
I saw as the Word of God
Or more appropriately,
As a Thought from the Light-
A thought from the Great Mind
That emerged as a vibration or sound
And descended out of the Light
And into the darkness

Immediately
The chaos that was the darkness began to calm
And orderly Life
Took hold in our World

In my vision
This seemed to happen in an instant
But then again
I think it may have taken eons
Of our time

This command, the Word of God
Is called many things-
The Great Om or Aum
The Amen or Amin
For the sound IT makes

The name doesn't matter
There is no understanding It

Whatever you call It
It is the vibrational command that came forth
(And still comes forth)
From the Great Mind
Maintaining all that is
In intelligent order

It, the Aum, is the Intelligent instruction
Behind our Laws of Nature
Behind our Laws of Science

It, the Word of God
Is the Laws of Nature,
The Laws of Science

Om *is* gravity, attraction, repulsion
Evolution

Om is the command
For this World to be orderly
And set in Its functions

Om *is* the rules
That govern this World

Though our world is duel,
Both male and female
The Light ITself is not

IT is One
Neither male nor female

Our world had to be duel
For there to be Life
And movement
And experience

If there were only One
There would be no experience
Or exploration
Or creation

The Light is One
Yet contains within IT all opposites
Which we perceive
With our minds

The Light is both the positive
And the negative
The Yang and the Yin
The Alpha particle
And the Omega particle
Yet through this collaboration
Between the two extremes
Life is created
And experienced

IT, God, Science
Is the ultimate Source
Of this Energy

Which creates Life
And is made orderly
Through the Great Om

The Light is alive-
IT is an Entity
Beyond our capacity to understand

IT is a living Intelligence
A living Consciousness or Awareness
A living Soul
And Immortal

IT does not age
For Consciousness does not age
Awareness does not age-
IT cannot

Our bodies can age
And may block the expression of Awareness
But Awareness itself, Consciousness, Soul...
These things do not age
They cannot

The Light is an Energy
And as such
IT can never be created
Nor destroyed,
IT can only change forms
And that is what has happened here

That is how our World was formed
And your body and mind as well

IT was never created
And IT can never die
IT just is
And IT always has been

IT created this World
And you
From ITs own essence-
A simple change in form
Of ITs own being

It follows then
That because IT is a form of Energy
That can never be destroyed
That the Universe, and you
Who are composed of that same Energy
But in a slightly different form
Are immortal as well

It follows even further then
That every single thing within this Universe
Being composed of a slightly different form
Of ITs Energy
Is alive and immortal as well

Since the inception of this World
There has not existed a single thing
That was not alive

Or that could die

There is not
Or ever has been
And never will be
Anything in the Cosmos that is dead
Or that can die

All things may change form
But there is no death

If you can grasp this
Lets move on,
For the next part
Is most sensational-

The Universe Itself is a Living Being
A conscious Life Form
And every part of It
As well

Can you grasp this?
This may be hard to comprehend!

The Universe ITself is a being
A living thing-
Alive
A sentient Entity

Think of It as a giant person
Though that is not quite true

But just like a person
The Universe is a living Entity
Conscious of Itself
Completely cognizant and aware

It is composed
Of smaller groups of living Entities
Including solar systems, and galaxies
And you

The little parts of the Living Cosmos
Are just like the cells and tissues and organs and systems
That make up your own body

Each cell and tissue and organ
That composes the totality of you
Are alive in and of itself as individual parts
Yet at the same time, composing the body
Of the larger organism
That is you

The Cosmos works the same way

It is alive-
It is a Being, an Entity
That is comprised of smaller parts
And every one of those parts,
Every single part
Is alive

Every single part

Is embued with the Force of Life, with Soul
And ordered into precision
By the Word of God,
The Great Om

We literally live and move and have our being
Within a living Cosmos
As if we were ITs cells
And our suns and planets were ITs atoms
Making up larger and larger Life Forms
Which eventually compose the entire body
Of the Living Cosmos Itself

Each solar system is an an atom
Each galaxy as a tissue
Each clump of tissue is as an organ
And so on
Yet each individual part is alive
Conscious and aware
And immortal

This Universe is teeming with Life!
The World is alive!
It is a living being!
The same as you!

The Cosmos is the whole
That contains the individual parts
That composes Its body
And every single inch
Is imbued with Life Force,

The Holy Spirit
And made orderly
By the Word of God,
Or Om

Everything in this Universe
Is completely saturated with Life
Which, through the Laws of Science and Nature
As directed by the Great Om
Makes the World orderly
And meaningful

First and foremost
Is IT, the Light
The Great Mind, the Father
The Great I Am
Awareness ITself, Consciousness
Whatever THAT is-
Immortal
Unaging
Without beginning or end

Second is the Great Cosmos- the Son
The Living Entity
That we know as the Universe

Within the Son
Is the Great Generator
Composed of the Positive and the Negative
The Alpha and the Omega
The Yang and the Yin

Which, through the friction
Of attraction and repulsion
Supplies the Life Force
Or Holy Spirit
That animates our Living World-
Every single piece of It

The Word of God, the Great Om
The Amen or Amin,
Brings order to this animation
And direction
And meaning

We knew as a child
That every single thing
In this World was alive
Didn't we?
We were closer to IT then

We simply grew up
And forgot

CHAPTER FIVE

If you have lost sight
Of the Mystery of Life
Then try to wrap your head around
The conundrum of time-
For time is not quite
What you think it is

Time is indefinite, elusive, evasive
And ill-defined
Its borders are blurred and puzzling
Its cadence is unclear and ambiguous

Time is not the absolute entity
You believe it to be
But instead it is an enigma, clouded,
Inexplicable

Everything from the perception of time
Within your head
To the actual movement of time
In the physical world

Is relative
And changing

Time is an illusion
That only seems to exist

Time is a construct of this World
Born of the constant movement
Of all things in this world
Through space

This movement is what allows
For the perception
Of a linear sequence of events

Everything in this world
Is in a state of constant motion
From atoms to galaxies
From thoughts to emotions

It is because of this motion
That time seems to move forward
In a linear manner,
And at a constant rate-
But this is not actually so

There is no set cadence
To the march of time

There is no constant rate
Or set rhythm

To how fast or slow time moves forward
Or seems to move forward

Our perception of time can change
Can it not?
Depending on circumstances

Surely you have noticed
That time seems to progress more slowly
As a child
But faster and faster
As we age

Surely you have noticed
That time progresses slowly
When you are unhappy
And much quicker
When you are not

Time perception
Is merely a creation of the mind
That is manipulable and distortable
Under certain circumstances

Furthermore
Time's pace changes
In the physical world as well

The faster an object moves
The slower time progresses
While the slower an object moves

The faster time will progress

Two objects moving at different speeds
Experience time differently,
At a different rate

This is measurable
Not just perception

If an object were able
To travel at the speed of Light
Time would cease to exist completely
As it does within the Light
Which exists in the realm
Beyond this World

Smaller objects also experience
A different perception of time
As compared
To larger objects

Time to a small unit of life, like a fly
Passes quickly
While for a larger unit of life, like a whale
Time passes more slowly

What to humans may seem
Like vast stretches of time
To the Entity that is the Universe
That same period of time
Is as if but a day

Even more of a conundrum
Is the fact that from our point of view
Something seems to happen
Then something else happens
Then something else-
There seems to be a linear progression
To the procession of time

One minute seems to follow the next
One moment comes before
And another moment comes after

Yet time is actually circular
Measured by the rotation of celestial objects
Around fixed points

Time is a circle, not a line
With no definite point
That comes before or after another

Lines have a start and a finish
But circles do not

Circles have no beginning
No middle or end
There are only points along the way
And each point has a point before and after it-
There is no set beginning
Or end

Pick a beginning, there is a point before it

Pick an end, there is a point after it

Where is the starting point to a day?
Where is the finish?
We choose 12 am as the starting point
And 11:59 pm as the finish
But these are just arbitrary points
That we choose for convenience-
A necessity for the measurement
Of what we perceive as time

The same goes
With the measurement
Of weeks and years
Decades and centuries
And every other, much longer
Measurement of time-
Many of which
You are not yet aware of

As the cycle of the day repeats
So does the cycle of the week
And the month
And the year
And the decade
And the century
All the way out to measurements
You cannot yet fathom

Time is an endless cycle-
Repeating in never-ending rhythms

Coming around again and again and again
Without end

Cycles of time you cannot comprehend repeat
And repeat
And repeat
As if they were the great inhalation
And exhalation
Of of the Universe Itself

Where is the start to time?
Where is the end?
Where is the past?
Where is the future?

There is no start or end to time-
It is a circle

And there is no past or future either
There is only now-
There is only a point on the circle
That represents the current position

If you say that the point before
The current point on the circle
Is the past
Then what happens if you go back far enough
Around the circle?
You end up ahead of your current position-
You end up in the future

If you say that the point after
The current point on the circle
Is the future
Then what happens if you go forward far enough
Around the circle?
You end up behind your current position-
You end up in the past

The past, the present and the future
All simultaneously exist,
Separated only
By the perception within our minds
Which divide events
Into separate happenings

Fully comprehending
The absolute enigma of time
Should awaken your zeal
For the absolute mystery
That is this World

Concentrating on this mystery
Is a path to an awakening
That you cannot yet imagine

It is a path to obtaining a glimpse
Beyond the veil of this World
Into Eternity
Where time does not exist at all

The next realm is right here

Right now
Just before you,
And it is a place beyond time-
A place of Eternity,
Which is defined
Not as unending time
But rather as a lack of time
As we know it

Time in this realm is but an illusion
Though a very stubborn one indeed

CHAPTER SIX

The Universe around us all
Is as the body
Of the Consciousness
That we call God
Which lives beyond
And emanates through
This realm

This Great Light
Nourishes each life form
With Consciousness and Awareness,
With Soul and Energy
And movement-
Each in proportion to its standing
On the scale of being

A fly does not have
The same level of Consciousness
As a human, for example
And therefore does not receive
The same degree of Mind

As that human

And the human
Does not have the same level of Consciousness
As the Cosmos Itself
And therefore does not receive the same degree
Of Mind
As the Cosmos

As the Consciousness of Life
Bathes our Souls with Awareness
So too does the light of our sun
Bathe our World with nourishment,
Bringing life
To all things on our planet

In this way
Our sun and its rays
(And all suns
And all rays from each sun)
Are as if a physical manifestation
Of the Great Light of Conciousness,
The Light of Awareness,
That enlivens our Souls

Our sun is the visible form of light
That we *can* see
Representing the invisible form of Light
That we *cannot* see
(Except through the Mind's eye
During efforts of silence

And deep concentration)

The light of the sun
Reminds us of the presence
Of the Light of Consciousness
Within and throughout this World-
The immaterial Light of pure Energy
That we cannot yet see

As such
Our sun is an image
Of that which we call God-
An Earthly reminder
Of the Great Light
That imbues this World
With its existence

As our sun
Nourishes our physical bodies
Its unseen counterpart
Nourishes our Minds with Consciousness

This is why
So many cultures
Have worshipped the sun as a god-
For the sun is the physical manifestation
And embodiment of the Great Light
That we cannot see
Which so nourishes our Souls
And gives us our Life
And our Being,

Our Awareness
And our identity

CHAPTER SEVEN

God, The Universe and Humankind
Are the three great Entities
In order of Greatness

All are One
Yet also made up
Of many parts

Each Entity
Is greater
Than the sum of ITs parts

God is God
IT is also the Universe
And everything in It-
Seen and unseen

All that is
All that exists
In this World or the next

Whether visible or not
Exists within IT
Whatever IT is

But the Light as a Whole
Is greater than the summation
Of all the individual parts

The Whole of the Light is One
And a Consciousness
Beyond all that we know

The Universe is also made up
Of many parts

The Universe is a living Entity
Created by the Light
Complete with Soul, and Consciousness-
It is a Being, and aware

It is made up
Of solar systems and galaxies
Suns and stars and quasars
Nebulae and black holes

These things are as the atoms
And cells and tissues
Organs and systems
Of the Entity
That we know
As the Universe

As with the Light
The summation of Its parts
Add up to a greater Being
With a far greater Consciousness
Than the mere addition
Of Its individual pieces
Could explain

Man too is made up
Of many parts-
From organs and bodily tissues
To cells
All the way down to atoms
And beyond-
Each smaller unit coming together
To form larger and larger units
Of matter and consciousness
Until the entire Entity
Is formed

Once again
The totality of the Entity of man
Is greater than the mere summation
Of its individual parts

God, the Universe and Humankind
Are the three Great Entities
Of existence as we yet know it

In that order

CHAPTER EIGHT

When the Great Light of Consciousness
(For lack of a better name)
Created the Universe
IT was well pleased
For ITs creation was beautiful and perfect
And IT loved It as ITs child

But there was no one
To share It with
So IT created humankind
In ITs own image

The Light created humankind
Out of ITs own Mind-
Out of a Thought

At first humankind was just a thought,
We had no bodies

We were Souls, Minds
We were Energy only, as the Light is Energy

We were Eternal and Spiritual
As is the Light
From whence we come-
And we existed in perfect peace
Within the Garden of Eden, so to speak

But then human Souls saw Creation
In all Its wonder and splendor-
And It was beautiful and perfect, majestic

And we wanted to experience
That mysterious realm
Of beauty and enchantment

We wanted to create
And to learn and to experience and to explore
To roam Creation
And to add our own unique verse
To the Book of Life
That is earthly existence

So God gave us a mortal body
Made up of the elements of the Universe
And we descended into form
And forgetfulness-
We have forgotten
Our true Nature

We had left the Garden of Eden

If we had not

We would have known only peace
For that is all we knew
In our original form

To experience
And to know happiness
We must also know sadness,
To experience triumph
We must experience failure

So we left the Garden of Eden
To experience this World

As we experience
And live
And learn and explore
And roam and create
The Great Light of Consciousness within us
Experiences this World as well,
Through us

We are here, we exist
First, to tend to Creation

Man is the dominant life form on earth
And as such
We are the caretakers of this world-
We are here to look after
Those forms of life
That are lesser than we are

We are here
To take care of the earth
And its inhabitants
As our Father
Takes care of us

We are secondly here
To explore and experience
And to add to Creation-
It is what we yearn to do
It is what we are here to do
And the Great Consciousness
Does not consider Creation complete
Until our unique part is added

We are here to add to the beauty
Of ITs creation
And we are doing this
Through the sciences and the arts,
Through philosophy
And through our relations
With each other

Each of us
Is capable of adding something unique
To Creation
Something particular
That only we can give,
For we are each special

There is no other like you

In all the World-
In all the history
Of the World

There is no other person
And never has been another person
That can add
What each of us specifically can
To this World

We each have something
That only we can give

Lastly
We are here to awaken,
To remember our divinity

Alchemy is a term
Used by many
To describe this awakening

This term is used
By some with a lesser understanding
To indicate the conversion
Of a base metal
Like lead
Into a higher and purer metal
Like gold

But this is only symbolic-
Symbolic of the conversion

Of something primitive and crude
Into something grand and special,
And pure

Through the burning off
Of all that is of lower nature and base
Something more precious is created,
Like turning lead into gold

Real Alchemy
Is a process of the Mind
Not a path to riches
In Worldly terms

Instead
Alchemy is a path
To something much grander-
The conversion of a base human being
Who is only concerned
With his or her own life
And selfish and individual needs
And with the pursuit of riches
Into something much more sublime-
A being concerned about the welfare of all
And a being who remembers
From whence he or she has come

When we treasure the things
Of this world
And only serve ourselves
We are treasuring those things

That can be taken away from us
Or used up
Causing us to suffer greatly

But when we start living
Not only for ourselves
But also for others as well
We place our hearts
Within a treasure
That can never be used up
Or taken away

When we have forgotten
Our true identity
And only identify with this body
We become timid and fearful,
For the body dies-
It has an end

But we are not our bodies-
We are beyond this World

At death we remain,
Only our body dies
And is returned to the soil

Our Consciousness is an Energy
Which can never be destroyed

When we come to remember this
Our suffering ceases

For what could bother you in the least
If you knew- if you remembered
That you were eternal
And could not be harmed?

What could harm you in the least?
The loss of a little money?
Not getting that new house?
Cancer?

These things are as nothing
And if you awaken
You will know this,
And you will no longer be moved
By the riches and other trivial things
Of this World
That come and go

Nor will you be moved
By loss
And ill health
And disease

You will instead develop a taste
For the deeper riches
Of the Infinite
Which never fade
And which you already possess
But have forgotten

Remember,

Or if you cannot remember
At least try to have faith,
And then you will suffer no more
As this World spins around you
Creating events
That sometimes seem to go in your favor
And sometimes seem to go against

For you will know
That you are just visiting this World
For a blink in time
And cannot be harmed

CHAPTER NINE

Humankind is the only life form on Earth
That can contemplate its Divinity
And ponder its purpose on earth
Which makes us very special

Our bodies are created
From the dust of the Universe
But our Minds are created
In the likeness of God-
Whatever God may be

Do other animals, insects and life forms
Not have bodies and minds as well?

Yes they do
But not to the degree
That humans do

The lesser life forms
Have more primitive bodies
And lesser levels

Of Consciousness and Awareness-
They have lesser levels of Mind

They cannot fathom
What humankind can fathom,
They cannot dream and imagine and create
As you and I can

And they cannot ponder
The Great Beyond

They cannot see
Beyond the Great Veil
Nor do they know
That such a thing exists

Only humankind
Has this ability

Humans are dual-
We have a body
And we have a Mind,
But not just any mind-
We have a Mind created
In the likeness
Of God's,
Capable of similar feats
As God's-
Creating and imagining
And enjoying an Awareness
Above the lesser life forms

What other life form
Creates as we do
For the mere pleasure
Of creating something beautiful?

Can any other life form
Imagine as we do?
Forming new ideas
And bringing Life to those ideas
In the science
And the arts

Can other life forms
Explore the Universe
With their Minds alone
Or even know this is possible?

Humans can create new Worlds
In their Minds
And bring those Worlds to life
In books and films

Humans can ponder other Worlds
In this Universe
And create means
To study them
And visit them

With spaceships
Humans have begun to explore
Out beyond the Earth

And with telescopes
Humans have even been able
To view all the way back
To the timeless birth
Of this World

What other life form on Earth
Can do such things?

What other life form on Earth
Can contemplate the Great Beyond
As we can?
Or awaken?
Or even know
These things are possible?
Or exist?

Of all the life forms on earth
Humans are the highest

We are both Earthly
And Divine-
The link between this World
And the next

Humans are even beyond the gods
That previous humans believed in-
For those gods
Had only Souls
But no bodies

Humans have both

All life forms have Souls
All life forms possess the Life Force
But only humans have progressed
To our level
Of Awareness and Consciousness

Humans are as if gods
To the other forms of life
On Earth

As such
We have dominion
Over this World
Which means
That we are as parents
To all that is below us

We are the caretakers
Of this world

When we take care
Of the earth
And its inhabitants
We are partaking
In the will of God
Who created It all

Why would the Light,
The Intelligence of this World

Create with Love
Such a place
Only for us to raid and rape IT's creation
And all Its resources
And all Its other life forms
Only for our own
Individual and personal gain?

Humankind is truly a marvel
Worthy of such wonder and awe-
Powerful beyond our own conceptions
Capable of such beauty
But also such horror

The job of a human
Is to love all that is below us
As we are loved
By all that is above us

We not only receive
The Light of the Divine
But we are able to give IT as well
Which is what we are meant to do

We are to serve this World
And all Its inhabitants-
To rise above our lower nature,
Selfish and greedy
Egotistical and narcissistic,
And to awaken to our Higher Nature

CHAPTER TEN

As we were created from the Light
And given Life
We were also given the ability
To create new Life as well-
Complete with a human Soul!

Can you comprehend
The enormity of this gift?
Can you see the Miracle?!

The act of union
Is a sacred matter
For sex is more than a mere physical act-
It is a spiritual union,
A rejoining of what was once One
But is now Two

In the timeless beginning,
The One split
And divided into the positive and the negative
The yin and the yang

The male and the female

IT did this
So that there could be separation
Allowing for experience-
For without separation
There would only be the One
And to experience
There must be something else-
Something outside of yourself

If you were whole
You would lack nothing
You would need nothing
There would be little
For you to experience

So the split had to occur
And it did
And the two sides were born

Each of the two Energies, now separate
Craves its other half-
Each side is incomplete on its own
And yearns for the other

We long to be whole again,
We long to be complete

Without the other half
We are each only half

Of the totality
Of the Whole
That we once were
And wish again to be

We hunger for that completion,
We ache for that which we lack
And we are attracted strongly
To the other-
For such is the power
Of our desire
To be One

When the male and the female come together
The energies unite
Like the positive and the negative sides
Of a magnet
And thus is the process of the separation
That occurred in the beginning
Reversed

The two halves become whole-
There is a uniting of flesh *and* Energy
Separation ceases and we become unified
And our yearning is satisfied

It is a temporary union
And not complete,
But powerful nonetheless

The re-union of the male and the female-

The re-union of the positive and the negative
Through the act of physical and emotional connections
Represents the reversal
Of the process of separation
That started this World

The intensity of the attraction
Between the male and the female
Is an absolute testament
To the insatiable yearning in our Soul
To be united

And the intensity
Of the explosion of feelings-
Both emotional and physical
During the unification
Is a testament as well
To the absolute desire of the union
Where the sum of the two parts
That come together
Is far greater
Than the mere summation
Of the individual parts

As pondering the Light
Is one way to pierce the veil
And see beyond this World
So too is the attraction
Between the male and the female
Another way-
Sex is a path

To experiencing the joy of being One
If you are able to recognize it
As such

What is Life?
We don't even fully comprehend what It is
Or how It can possibly be
Yet we can create It
Through the union
That we so crave

We can actually create a life form
Complete with a fully formed body
And an immortal Soul!
Whatever that is

We can create a new Consciousness,
A new Awareness
A new Intelligence
Unique in all the World

We have the capacity
To create a being
Unlike any
That have ever walked this Earth

Lower life forms
Crave union as well
But are unable to comprehend
Anything beyond their cravings-
They cannot understand

The full power
Of the union, or what it represents

Nor do they realize this union
As the source of reproduction

Life is a ripening process-
As a fruit emerges green and unripe
Unfit to be eaten
So too are all life forms
That inhabit earth
Unripe spiritually,
At least initially

As all life forms live
And experience life
They begin to ripen-
They begin to expand their Consciousnesses
They begin to catch on
They begin experiencing higher and higher levels
Of comprehension and awareness

Human Consciousness is the pinnacle
Of consciousness and awareness
And when a human being ripens
It is a thing of beauty

It is like the caterpillar
That emerges from the cocoon
As a butterfly

When we are fully ripe
We return once more
To the pure Consciousness and pure Awareness
From whence we began-
Leaving this world behind
As a butterfly leaves the cocoon

This cycle, this ripening process
Starts with the dull existence
Of a lower organism
Who has little comprehension or awareness
Of anything other than survival
And progresses over time
Until eventually that organism gains comprehension

Little by little
That comprehension grows
Into higher and higher levels of consciousness
Until finally that organism takes human form

From the human form
And from human Mind
That life form eventually reaches a level
Of comprehension
In which he or she
Is able to awaken

When that human awakens
He or she is reborn
Back into awareness
Of the ONE

This is the destiny
Of all forms of life

We all make this trip eventually

Some arrive quicker than others
But that makes no difference

If you cannot *yet* appreciate
The miracle of the union
Of the male and the female form
Or yet understand or appreciate
Any of the other information
Being put forward for you
It is ok-
You are not lost
Or broken beyond repair

You simply do not *yet* see or comprehend
The Great Mystery
That is Life

But you will

CHAPTER ELEVEN

There seems to be
A common argument
Over whether our lives are ruled
By destiny
Or by free will

The answer is both

If a man is born a thief-
That is to say
If it is in his nature to steal
And that person
Has been a thief for fifty years
It is not a stretch to say
That that person
Will be a thief
For the rest of his life

Stealing is in his nature
And he will do
What his nature dictates

In this way
His destiny is sealed-
He will succumb to the fate
Of his nature

If another man is an addict-
That is to say
That this person has an addictive nature
And has been an addict
For many years
It is not a stretch to say
That that person
Will most likely be an addict
For the rest of his life

It is in his nature
To be addicted

His destiny is set
His fate is sealed

Unless...

Unless he is able
To rise above his own nature
And free himself from the slavery
He has given himself over to

His nature owns him-
It dictates automatically
His reactions to all things he will face

And therefore dictates
The direction of his life

Each of us has a particular nature
Each of us has a personality
A way of doing things and reacting to things
That is unique
Only to ourselves

The die of the Universe is cast
We cannot decide or control
What issues we face in life,
But we do have a choice
On how to deal with them

Life is not what comes at you
But how you react
To what comes at you,
And very few of us
Are able to rise above our nature
And meet life head on,
Consciously choosing
The course of the direction
Of our own lives

We are capable
Of being the masters
Of our own lives,
For the majority of us though
Life is a reflex-
Automatic, set

Without thought or contemplation
To what we face

Our natures
Are our masters

For most of us,
Fate is sealed-
Destiny is set
And we will continue to get
What we have always gotten

If you are a fearful person
You will make fearful decisions
And react fearfully
To the external and internal
Dramas of life

If you are an angry person
You will make angry decisions
And react angrily
To all that you experience

Some of us will be destined to be successful
But only because
Those people have a nature
That will react well
To the events
That they are destined to face
In their lives

Others are destined to fail
For their reactions
Will not go well
With the events
They are destined to face
In their lifetime

In either event
Success or failure
Is simply luck of the draw-
The reactions of your nature
Combined with the scenarios
You are destined to face

Your life will play out predictably,
Where you end up
Will be near inevitable

But as you mature
As a human being
And grow in Mind and Intellect and Consciousness
You will come to see
That the reactions of your nature
Is not your only choice

How many times
Must you touch a hot stove
Until you realize
That it is not a good idea?

The sensation

Of touching the hot stove
Is a painful lesson
That teaches you
To choose differently

Even a lower animal
Will learn this lesson

Life makes you uncomfortable
When you make bad choices-
When will you stop
Making those choices?

You are free!
Not bound by your nature-
You are your own master
Not enslaved to anything else
Much less your own thoughts and emotions

As you cast your nature aside
You become free,
Completely free
To live intentionally-
To live as you wish

Do this
And you move beyond destiny
And into the realm
Of Free Will

It is our purpose as humans

To rise above our fate
And become masters
Of our own lives

As you do this
You will come to know
A different part of yourself-
A deeper part,
Beyond the body
And beyond the thoughts
That rise and fall-
Even beyond your instincts
And inborn nature

Your instincts
And inborn nature
Are of this World-
They come from the combined genetics
Of your parents,
But there is a part of you
Beyond even this
For it is from a time and a place
Before and beyond this World
And this incarnation

Fate and destiny
Have no power whatsoever
Over what lies
Within you
At your core

As you rise above your nature
And break free of its constraints
You will come to get a feel
For the Watcher within-
The real you
That exists
Beyond the reach
Of this World

CHAPTER TWELVE

Death is probably
The single greatest fear
That most living things face-
Yet it is also
An absolute certainty

There is no way
To avoid it

The second a thing is born
It immediately begins to age-
Every moment it grows and matures
And eventually begins a decline
That will end in death

From the moment you enter this World
You are making your way
Towards the end

This is simply the way
Of this fleeting World

Physical matter
That has come together
To form a living thing
Can only last so long
Before it begins to decay
And break back down
Into its original elements

From the highest life forms
To the lowest
From atoms and cells
To solar systems and galaxies
All things are in a constant state
Of flux-
Either growing towards maturity
Or declining
Towards death

It is our fate-
The fate of all things
In this World

Touch a thing
Then immediately touch it again-
The thing you touched the second time
Has alread aged
At least a little
From the first time you touched it-
It is now a little closer
To death

We must learn to accept
The impermanence of this life
If we are to have
Even a moment's peace
In our minds

If we do not
We will suffer needlessly,
And constantly

But beneath it all-
Beneath this impermanence,
There is a Permanence-
Beyond all this death
There is Life

There is an Intelligence
There is a Consciousness,
An Awareness
That is not a physical entity
Doomed to decline and decay
Like the things of this World

Instead
It is as some sort of Energy
Which can never be destroyed
But can only change
From one form
To another

This Energy, whatever IT is

Is a timeless Intelligence-
A Force
Behind the workings
Of this world

How do atoms
Stay together?

How do magnets know
To be attracted
To each other?

How does gravity
Know how to work?

How do planets know
How to rotate and revolve
Around other objects
In a predictable and orderly fashion?

This Intelligence,
Whatever IT is
Is the answer
To those questions

IT is the Force
Behind the cohesion of atoms
And the attraction of magnets

The Force
Behind the pull of gravity

And the rotation of planets

The things of this World
Are physical,
Doomed to decay and death
But the Laws behind
The workings of this World
Are not-
And neither is the Energy,
The Intelligent Force
Behind the workings
Of this World

Finding the Permanent
In the impermanent
Is the reward
Of your spiritual or scientific quest

Find the Impermanent
And anchor to IT
And you will suffer no more

What could shake your peace
Or state of mind
In the least
If you knew
That you were eternal
And beyond harm-
Only carrying this body
As a turtle carries its shell?

Birth is not the beginning
For the Human Soul
Nor is death the end
Of our Consciousness

So what fear is there?
What could possibly
Shake your peace?

Our Mind, our Awareness
Is not physical-
Doomed to the same fate
As the material body housing It

Instead
Our Mind, our Awareness
It is an Energy,
A Consciousness,
That is as indestructable
As the Great Awareness
From whence it came,
Only housed temporarily
In an impermanent, transient and fleeting home

The body, well-worn
Disintegrates back into dust
For that is the nature
Of physical matter

But the Mind lives on,
Consciousness lives on

Unscathed, undamaged
For that is the nature
Of Energy-
It is indestructible

There is no need to fear death
Simply seek the Permanent
Within this impermanent and fleeting World
And you will see

CHAPTER THIRTEEN

Birth is not the beginning
Of the Human Soul
Nor is death the end
Of your Consciousness

What you are *is* a Consciousness
That existed long before
You incarnated into your current body,
And will exist long after
This current body
Has returned to the earth

This teaching
Is every bit as much
A scientific reality
As it is
A spiritual belief
For the body is physical,
It is mortal-
Subject to all matter of ills
And eventually subject

To decline, decay and death
As per the rules of matter
In this World

But Consciousness
Is an Energy
And as such
Is immune to such things
As decline and decay and death
As we also know
From the study
Of science

As humans
We are curious-
We grow and we explore and we learn,
And as we do
Our understanding and our perception
Grows and expands as well

As our Mental capacity increases
We mature as humans
And eventually, we come to understand
More and more
And we come to perceive things
That we were not even aware of
Before

With this progression
In the growth of our Awareness
Tends to come a growth

In our compassion
For all living things,
As well as a focus
That now extends
Beyond ourselves alone-
Beyond our opinions,
Beyond our own immediate
And self-centered concerns

This is the ripening process
That humans evolve through
Over time-
And it is one of the purposes
For our existence
In this realm

We as humans
Are evolving, transforming
From a base, primitive human being
Full of ignorance and arrogance,
Full of anger and self focus and ego
Into a being of great intelligence-
A being of increased perception and awareness
And a being of great compassion

At the death of the body
The Mind is simply freed
From its physical container

From there
The Mind is drawn to the next realm

A realm that is here
Right in front of you
Right now
But exists at a different vibrational level-
A different level of Energy,
One that you cannot yet see
While trapped inside
The body

Like sound waves
That vibrate at a frequency
That you cannot hear
Or colors
That exist outside the spectrum
Your eyes can discern
So too is the next realm
Just before you
Yet vibrating at an Energetic frequency
You cannot as yet perceive

After death of the body
If the Mind has matured,
If the Mind has ripened
And grown in Intellect and Love
And become strong enough
To exist in the next realm-
That realm is your next home

Your Mind is drawn into it
As a magnet is drawn
To its mate,

For your Mind
And the next realm
Will vibrate at similar rates-
They will be
Of similar frequencies

Just as we
Were developed for this current world
In the womb,
So too
Are we being developed
For the next world
Within these bodies

Just as we emerged
From the world
Of our mothers womb
Into this world,
So too
Will we emerge
From the world of these bodies
Into the next

If the Mind has not yet matured
Or ripened enough
It will not yet be strong enough
To survive in the next realm-
Its vibrational frequency
Will be too low
To stay in the next realm,
So it is drawn back down

Into another earthly existence

This is not a punishment-
There is no punishment,
Only growth

That particular Mind
Simply needs more experience
It needs to ripen and mature
A bit more

All living things
Have gone through this process
And continue
To go through this process

All will eventually make it-
All ripen and mature over time

The base humans
Of this world,
Angry and selfish
Egotistical and deceptive,
Are future saints-
They are simply still
At a lower level
Of existence
At this moment

Even in the heavenly realms
Growth continues

From the earthly existence
To the heavenly realms
The physical body is shed
But there is more to be shed
In the end
Than just the physical body

In the heavenly realm
There are many levels
And each level
Is made of an Energy
That vibrates at a slightly higher frequency
Than the one before

As we exist in these realms
We live as we have on earth
And our Souls continue to ripen and mature

As they do-
As our Souls mature further and further
And shed and cast off
All that is not Light
We vibrate at higher and higher frequencies
And move upward and onward
Into the higher Energetic
And heavenly realms

When we have matured completely
And shed off all that is not Light,
All that is not Consciousness,
All that is not Love,

Then we rejoin
The Great Light
From whence we came
And we become
As gods

This Great Light
Whatever IT is
Resonates and oscillates
At such a high frequency
That it seems as if
It is not moving
At all

IT seems as if
IT is completely still

CHAPTER FOURTEEN

The true pity
Of this life
Is that we as humans
Have the ability
To rise above
A mere physical existence
During our incarnation
In this physical plane
But seldom do

We can,
Here and now
Rise above
And live beyond
This body and this ego
We take to be ourselves
And thus be liberated
From the many ills of this World

Most of us live our days
Ignorantly filled to overflowing

Only with the temporary pleasures
And endless dramas of this World

We want more money
We want more social status
We want this person to like us
We want our friends to not like
Those that we do not like

We tend to live our lives
From beginning to end
Filled full of our own egos
Filled full of our own opinions
And so completely attached
To our bodies
And the pleasantries and dramatic events
Of this World
That we never even know
That more exists

The things of this World are nice
They are for you to enjoy-
Go partake!
Explore!
Learn!
Enjoy!

But most of us do not enjoy
Do we?

For most of us take our ego

And our body
And our belongings
And our dramas
To be the essence
Of our lives-
We take these things
To be Who and What we are

We become so attached
And so addicted
To our egos
And to our bodies
And to our possessions
And to our daily happenings
That we think we *are*
Those things

The fate of our happiness
Then becomes tied
To the fate of those things

When our bodies are good
And our egos are good
And we have possessions
And drama we like,
Then we are happy

When any of those things go wrong
We suffer

Yet *we* are meant

To be the master,
Not the slave

We are meant
To have a body and an ego and possessions
Not become enslaved by them

We are meant to possess
The pleasantries
Of this World,
Not to be possessed
By them

We as humans
Have the ability to learn
And comprehend
And see
Beyond these things

We have the capacity
To lift the veil
And discover
That though we are *in* this World
We are not *of* this World

Until such time,
We will continue to suffer

We will suffer
When we do not get what we want

We will suffer
When we get what we didn't want

We will even suffer
When we get exactly what we do want

How can this be?

It is due to the fear
Of eventually losing
Whatever it is
That we wanted
And have now obtained

In addition,
Once a desire is obtained
We still are not satisfied-
We always want more don't we?
We can never get or have enough

The things of this World are nice
And for our enjoyment
But they are fleeting and empty-
There is no substance to them,
They do not fill your cravings

The more you get, the more you want
And your addiction for them grows,
Devouring your happiness
Without mercy-
As all addictions do

The transient pleasantries of this World
Will never satisfy you-
They will never fill you up

But there *is* a Treasure
That may seem subtle,
But once experienced
Will fill you to the brim,
And you will never want
For another thing

This Treasure
Is Knowledge-
A Knowledge
That will set you free
And lead you to a peace of mind
You cannot imagine

This Treasure
Once obtained
Can never be taken away

Unlike the things of this World
It can never grow old
Or decline or decay
Or die

The more of this Treasure you want,
And the more of this Treasure you ask for
The more of IT is offered,
Yet IT can never be exhausted

Once you obtain this Treasure
You will be free-
You will be reborn
You will be awake,
You will be enlightened

You will be liberated
From the cares of this World
Into an existence
Devoid of suffering

You will be able
To enjoy your body
And your ego
And all the pleasantries and dramas
Of this World,
But you will no longer be attached to them
And possessed by them

The fate of your peace of mind
Will no longer be tied
To the fate
Of these temporary pleasures

You will be free to enjoy this World
The way it was meant to be enjoyed-
Without a care in the World

If you knew the truth-
That nothing could harm you in the least
Or affect you in any way

What could hold you back?
Or shake your peace of mind?

Until then
Your happiness and peace of mind
Will be tossed without mercy
On a tumultuous sea
Of your own addictions
To transient and empty
Passions and desires

It is a fools game-
And of your own making

What you really want
Are not those things
That you seem so attracted to,
But the Truth
Behind those things

All desire
Is really desire
For this Truth

We all have this desire-
We simply get confused
As to where
To find IT

Use the immense power
Of your Mind

To seek the Truth-
Make this the main focus
Of your desires

Simply having the desire
To find Truth
And making any real effort
To find IT
Is enough
To set things in motion

For as we search for the Truth
IT seems to appear before us
In a million different
And unexpected ways

The power of the Mind is such
That whatever you concentrate on
And make your desire
Starts coming into the view
Of your daily life

One hundred people
Can look at the same scene
And depending on their focus
Will notice one hundred
Different things

A new husband may see in a landscape
A perfect place to build a house
For his new family

An artist
May see the makings
Of a most perfect painting

A philosopher
May gain insight
Into a question
He had been stuck on

A mother
May see an area of danger
To her small child

A poet may find the inspiration
She had been seeking

And an entrepreneur
May see a venture
In which money can be made

All these things exist
In the same view
But what each of us sees
Depends on what each of us seeks

We each see
What we seek-
Our focus
Becomes our reality

Seek possessions

And we see their possibilities
All around us-
Seek the Truth
And everywhere you look
It starts to appear
Right before you

You start to recognize IT
In everything you see,
In everything you hear,
In everything you think

The sound of a bird
The laugh of a child
The hug of a friend-
Simple daily events,
A song,
A meal,
A comment by a friend-
In every scenario of life
You will begin to see IT,
Truth will begin to emerge
All around you,
And you will begin
To awaken

Eventually
The ultimate Truth will descend on you
And hit you like a load of bricks
Or a flash of lightening

To describe the event
Is futile-
IT is an experience
Beyond the comprehension
Of this World

But the realization
Is like looking for hours
At a puzzle picture
With a hidden image,
When all of a sudden
The hidden image
Comes easily and without effort
Into view

Suddenly IT is everywhere,
IT is in every single thing-
In fact
IT is all that is

IT is so obvious
And so close,
Right in front of our eyes-
But for so long
We simply didn't have the eyes yet
To see

We sought drama
And we sought possessions,
And that is what we perceived

But now that we have sought IT
We have been awakened to IT
And Life
And Truth
Has opened up before us
And lain at our feet

There is
With this
Such a Peace
That you have never known
Or can even imagine

This Peace
Is our birthright as humans
And our goal

CHAPTER FIFTEEN

Whatever God is
IT is beyond us
And beyond all suffering

IT enjoys this World
Yet is not attached
To this World

IT partakes
Of this World
Yet is not tied
To this World

ITs peace is unshakable,
And absolute

Would you like
To be this way?

If so,
Then emulate

God's ways

This is a great secret
So listen closely…

If you want to be a great businessman
Then find one,
Study his or her traits and behaviors
And copy them

If you want to be a great teacher
Or a great healer
Then find one
And study his or her ways
And make them your own

And if you want to be
A great philosopher
Then learn from the best
And follow suit

This is a little-known way
Of finding and obtaining
What you most want
And most desire
In life

If you have matured
To the point
That what you most want
Out of this World

Is to be free of its dramas
Then you must copy the behavior
Of That which *is* free,
You must copy the behavior
Of That which *is* beyond-
You must copy God

How do we go about
Emulating God?

God explores
And God creates

You too
Will be most happy
When you explore and create
As well

God allows us
To explore and create
And live our lives
The way we wish
To live our lives-
And we should grant
That same freedom
To others as well

Having our actions
Dictated by another
Is intolerable,
So why would we not allow

The same freedom to others
That we wish
For ourselves?

Trying to make another
Bend to our concept
Of how they should live their lives
Is futile, and agonizing-
Why would we do that
To ourselves?

God is merciful
Without fail,
And so should we be-
Even to those
Who have shown no mercy
To us

God is without judgement,
And shows no favoritism-
God makes the sun to shine
On the lives
Of both sinners and saints,
And makes the rain to fall as well
On the lives of both

If God is beyond judgement
Then we too should be

God Loves all that is,
Without any condition whatsoever,

And so should we-
Even our enemies

It is easy to love
The family and friends
We already love-
Real growth occurs
From loving
Everyone else

God gives and gives and gives-
Constantly and continuously

All there is
And all that you have
Is from God

Giving is God's nature
And so should it be yours
As well

God does all this giving
Without a moment's thought
Of recompense or reward,
And so should you-
Giving should be its own reward

God serves us all
As we should serve others
As well

Most of all
God *knows* ITself
To be
Not of this World

God knows
For a fact
That IT is a Consciousness
Playing and exploring
In this World,
Not a material thing
Of this World
That is doomed
To decline and to decay
And to death

God is thus free,
As you wish to be free,
Of the limitations
And fears
And trappings
Of this material World

As we act like God
We become like God

If we want to be free
As God is free
And liberated from the fears
And the dramas and the addictions
We think to be our reality,

Then we must emulate God-
We must become like God

Salvation depends
Not on how many pleasantries
You can obtain
In this Word-
Nor does it depend
On how well
Your ego is stroked

These things breed only greed
And misery,
Addiction and attachment

Salvation is not to be found either
In how well
You have memorized
Your favorite holy scriptures,
Or how loud you sing in church
Or how much you tithe

Instead
Becoming free,
Becoming a god among men
Is a matter of will-
Your salvation depends
On how close you have come
To being like God

CHAPTER SIXTEEN

In order to increase
The power of your Mind
And to open the doors
Of perception
That you may see
Beyond the veil of this World,
You must exercise your Mind
And expand your Consciousness
To a new level

Imagine that you are
A person
Of the opposite sex

Truly try to imagine

Can you put yourself
In their shoes?

Can you imagine
Their wants and needs

And desires?

Can you understand things
From their perspective?

Now imagine
That you are a person
Of another race
A person of another creed
A person of another color

Try to see things
From their beliefs and understandings-
Can you do it?

Now expand your Mind further,
Stretch It out a bit,
And try to imagine that you are you
Yet you are also
Every other person on earth
As well

Imagine you are the human race
As a whole

When in a group
Imagine that you are yourself
But also every person
In the group as well

Practice this regularly-

Keep trying
Until your Mind catches on
And becomes capable
Of such a feat

The Mind is a muscle
That must be worked
In order to grow

In order to increase the awareness
And perception of our Minds
We must break through the limits
Of regular consciousness
By constantly transcending the boundaries
That we assume to define
Our seemingly concrete existence

Imagine now that you are a dog
Or a cat
Or a bird,
Or any other animal
Of your choice

Can you do this?

Can you perceive life
From their perspectives?

Try to live
From the perspective
Of an ameba

Or a bacteria
Or a virus

How would things look to them?
What would be their motives?
What would their lives be like?
What do they feel?
What do they do?

Now let's expand further
And try to imagine
That you are every life form on earth

You are every single life form-
Humans and insects
Animals and microscopic creatures,
Plants, flowers and trees-
Any and everything that has life,
That is what you are

You are all life forms
All at once,
You are life forms
As a whole-
You are life forms
In general

How does it feel?
What do you see?

From this perspective

What do the individual wants and needs and desires
Of each life form seem like?
Do they seem important?
Do they seem frivilous?

Do the overall wants and needs and desires
Of Life as a unit
Seem more important?
Or do the individual wants and needs and desires
Of each individual Life Form
Seem more important?

Are the wants and needs and desires
The same on the larger and the individual scale?
Or do they contradict each other?

Now let's extend
Your imagination into space-
Imagine that you are the Sun
Or the moon
Or the stars

Or that you are the space
Between celestial objects

Imagine that you are our solar system
And every planet, moon, star and sun within it

Imagine now
That you are our solar system,
As before- but now you realize

That you are a living Entity-
Alive and conscious of Itself

Now image
That as the solar system
You are also like a single atom
In a much larger entity

Can you wrap your head
Around such an idea?
Keep trying-
The Mind will eventually adapt

Now imagine life
From the perspective
Of that larger entity,
Whatever It may be

How would Life look
To such a thing?
We see life
From a microscopic perspective
Compared to something that large-
What does It see?

What could be Its wants and desires
And needs?

Now imagine life
As both that entity
And all the smaller life forms

That make It up

Moving on
Try to imagine that you are the law of gravity
And the cohesion that holds
The Universe together

Next go microscopic
And imagine that you are an atom

Imagine that you are clumps of atoms
Forming a Life Form

Imagine that you are that Life Form
And also the billions of individual atoms
That come together
To form that Life Form

Now imagine
That you are every atom
In existence-
You are atoms
In general

Push your Mind further
And Imagine
That you are the Universe

Imagine that you are
Every living being
In the Universe-

From the smallest form of Life
To the Universe Itself
As an entity

Imagine your consciousness expanding
From one end of the Universe
All the way
To the other end

Imagine there being no beginning
To the Universe
And no end
In either direction

Hard to wrap your Mind around
Is it not?

Imagine that you exist
Before the physical World
Within the physical World
And after the physical World-
All at the same time

Imagine that you are
Right now
Unborn, in your mother's womb
Yet also young and old
And also dead
And beyond this realm-
All at the same time

Imagine that you have no beginning
And imagine that you have no end

Imagine that you created
The physical World,
But are also
A part
Of the physical World-
You are both creator
And part
Of your own creation

Imagine that you are the Life Force
That courses through Life-
Imagine that you *are* Life

Keep expanding
The reach of your Mind
And imagine that,
Like God
You are everywhere,
And at all times

Imagine that,
Like God,
You are all that is
And all that will ever be

Concentrate deeply
And often
On these things-

Make this your Mind's focus

Contemplate so intently
That you become unaware
Of all around you-
Become unaware
Of the existence of your own body

Concentrate so hard
That you forget
That you even exist

The human Mind is so powerful,
So unlimited,
So capable-
Beyond belief

Yet It is like a muscle-
With use it grows
With disuse it wilts

Give the Mind a thing to do,
Give it a focus-
A direction in which to grow,
And it will

Want to get good at chess
Or piano
Or physics?
Concentrate on these subjects-
Study them and practice them

Over and over and over
And with time
Your Mind will catch on
And master the subject
You have chosen

This is the science
Of the Mind-
This is how the Mind works,
And how to harness Its power
In the direction you wish

What *we* are concerned with
Is the expansion
Of the human Mind-
The expansion of Consciousness,
The opening of Awareness
And perception

That is the direction
That is the focus,
On which we wish
To direct our Minds

For we wish to see
Beyond the veil of this World

We wish to travel beyond suffering
And into Peace

We wish to have

The peace of God

At first this will be very hard-
Many of these ideas and concepts
Will be beyond
Your capabilities-
You will not be able
To wrap your head around
Many of them

But over time
Your Mind will strengthen,
Its abilities and capabilities will expand
And the exercises
Will become easier

The Mind will grow and expand
And as It does
Your understanding and perception
Of this World
And What is beyond
Will increase as well

You will begin to perceive
And to understand things
That up to this point
Have been a mystery,
Or not even perceptible
To you

For you did not yet have

The eyes with which to see
Nor the ears with which to hear
Them with

Like a puzzle picture
With a hidden image
That you have stared at for hours,
The image
Will open all of a sudden before you
And with ease

Or imagine it is like
Trying to remember the name
Of a famous person
But you cannot

Then days later
The name occurs to you
Out of the blue

The Mind
Does what you tell It to

If you tell It
To find you more temporary pleasures
And drama,
It will

If you tell It
To remember a famous person's name
Or find the hidden image

In a puzzle picture,
It will-
Even working on the solution
You requested
Underneath your awareness

And if you tell It
You wish to understand this World
And What is beyond
And you concentrate
On the task
And repeat it regularly
The Mind will rise
To the occasion

Those that have unlocked
The puzzle of Life
Have become free and complete-
They sit happily at the feet
Of the Great Mystery,
Watching in constant amazement
Without a care in this World

But be warned-
Such people
Are often thought crazy
By the masses-
They are laughed at and ridiculed and hated,
Even despised-
Some have been tortured
And put to death

The wisest among us
Have often had
To endure such fates

People fear
What we they do not understand,
And that fear
Breeds destruction

CHAPTER SEVENTEEN

The mass of people around you
Are not yet ready-
If they are exposed to these teachings
They will find little that interests them
Or that makes sense to them

At the next level
Will be people
Who are interested
In this topic,
And the teachings
Will make sense to them
To some degree,
But they are just not yet ready
To take their studies
To full fruition

Then there will be the very few
Who are ready-
The teachings for them
Will be exciting

And seem to be
What they have been waiting for
Their entire life

These people
Will become intent
On awakening,
The idea
Will occupy their Minds
On a regular basis

They will read and they will learn
And they will meditate and contemplate
And do whatever else it takes
To pierce the veil
And see beyond

Those that are not yet ready
Are not bad or evil,
Though they may seem like it
At times

They are often racist and sexist
Filled with hatred
And jealousy and anger

Their speech and their actions
Are often brash
And hurtful and violent as well

But there is no such thing as evil,

Only ignorance,
And the fear and anger that comes
From ignorance

As these people ripen
They will learn-
They will grow in Knowledge
And their Consciousness will expand

Eventually
They will put behind them
Their harsh and volitile ways,
Growing out of such actions
As a child
Grows out of his or her shoes

Growth past the dramas
And harsh opinions
And rash behaviors
And addiction to the temporary luxuries
And pleasures
Of this World
Is the fate
That awaits us all
At some point

In the past
These teachings
And others like them
Were guarded in secrecy

Torture and death
Were threatened
For those that revealed these secrets
To others

But this was not necessary
For these secrets guard themselves-
Only to those that are ready for them
Will they have any real meaning

Most people around you
Are still caught up
In the dramas and transient pleasures
Of this World

There is no use
To try and speed up their progression-
They will be ready
When they are ready

Until then
Let them be
And judge them not,
For you were once just as ignorant
And just as caught up in this World
As they are now

Making these teachings
A part of your daily life
Is hard
And an individual journey

That each person
Must take on their own

Until you fully awaken
It is very difficult to let go
Of the way
We are used to things being
And the way
We are used to doing things
And viewing things

It is also not easy
To break free from the thinking
Of the crowd,
Even when you know them to be wrong

So be patient
And be kind
To those
That are not yet ready
For the path-
You were once
One of them

If you are ready for The Path though,
Let nothing stand in your way-
For it may take great resolve
To break away
From Life
The way you now know it

And remember,
Most of all
That awakening or being reborn
Is an experience
That must be experienced
To understand,
Not merely words on a page
To be memorized, chanted
Or argued over

CHAPTER EIGHTEEN

I have done my best
To lead you,
By my example,
Beyond the veil
Of this World

I have given you
To the best of my ability
The knowledge I obtained
When I first awoke

I have even laid out the path
To the best of my ability
To liberation,
The way I achieved it

There is one more thing
I am going to try to do for you-
I am going to try and explain
The experience
Of enlightenment,

The experience
Of rebirth

I am going to try
And give you a sense
Of what it is like

Please keep in mind though
That awakening
Is an experience
For which
There truly are
No words

Any attempt
At description
Is feeble at best

That being said...

My mind had been focused
In deep concentration
As it had been
So many times before-
And I was wholly intent
In my focus

I was so deep in silence
And contemplation
That my senses had withdrawn
Or seemed suspended

And I traveled beyond my thoughts

My mind was alert
And clear
And my understanding
Seemed to surpass
Any clarity
I had ever known

All of a sudden
It was as if my Intelligence,
As if my Consciousness
Or Awareness
Had finally expanded
And grown
And stretched out
To the point
That the physical
And egotistical confines
That had contained It for so long
Were no longer adequate

My expanding Consciousness
Seemingly shattered Its borders
And broke free

Once free
My Consciousness seemed to explode,
Surging over and past Its previous borders-
Expanding instantaneously
In every direction forever-

There was nothing left to stop It,
There were no more borders
Whatsoever

My Mind, My Soul
Opened up before me

The Universe
Opened up
Before me

God
Opened up
Before me

I saw my Mind
I saw my Consciousness
I saw my Soul
And I saw
What we call God

The feeling, if it could be described
Was as if
My Mind had suddenly awakened,
And I was able to remember
What I had so long ago forgotten!

I had returned
To my home!

The liberation I felt

Could never be explained-
The Joy!
The Freedom!
The Peace!

I was no longer my body,
Nor was I my ego
Or the thoughts and emotions
I once took to be me

I was something similar
But deeper

I was still me-
I could still think and feel
And I still had identity,
But that identity had shed
All egotistical and bodily concerns

I saw
And I understood
And I remembered
Who and What I was,
And I saw
And I understood
From Whence I had come

I saw the Light
And IT made sense-
Everything made sense

I saw the Great Light of Intelligence
Penetrate everything

IT penetrated the physical World
And IT was the physical World

IT penetrated the mental World
And IT was the mental World

IT was the Laws of Nature-
And IT was Nature

IT was time
Yet IT was also beyond time

IT was everything-
There was nothing
IT was not

And all of that
Made sense-
Everything made sense

The Light of Concsiousness
Was so intense,
Brighter than any light
I had ever known-
IT was resplendant

IT bore deeply
Into every aspect

Of every single thing-
Nothing could resist
ITs illumination

IT shined into and through
Every single thing,
And IT was
Every single thing

Yet the intensity
Was not uncomfortable-
IT was the most Peaceful
Most welcome Glow
Your Mind could perceive

I had found the Source
And IT was bubbling with Life
And Light and Love,
And Intelligence
And Consciousness,
And IT penetrated
All that is
All that ever was
And all that ever will be

There was no escaping IT-
There was nothing but IT

IT was eternal
And boundless,
IT was all that existed

And I
And you
Were part of IT-
And made
In ITs likeness

And this made sense
As well

I wanted to give thanks
And to somehow pray
Or give praise,
But I realized
There was no need-
There was no me
That was separate from IT

Any praise
I could give
Would just be IT
Praising IT
Through me,
And I'm not even separate
From IT

I told you
This was hard to explain!

All I could do
Was sit
In silent reverence,

Filled with a Peace
I had never known

I was free...
I was home

I emerged from the vision
Changed completely-
Internally
I was no longer even a shadow
Of what I once was,
Yet to all who looked upon me
With physical eyes
I had not changed at all

They could only see
The outside of me,
They could not see
My Mind

How to explain this?
There is no way

When a man awakens, you see
IT is his Mind
That is reborn-
His body
Does not change

What I had become
Was invisible

To the human eye
But completely visible
To the Mind

Even though I still have physical eyes
And obviously can see with them
It is really with Mind
That I now
Comprehend and see,
For that is what I am

In fact,
IT seems as if
I now view the World
Not just through my Mind,
But through
The Great Mind

I now seem to witness
This World
Through God's Mind
And through God's understanding

I am no longer my body
And I am no longer my ego,
And I know this to be true-
I know it as a fact

I am now aware
That what I am
Is a Presence-

A Presence that is currently residing
Within my body

A Presence that expands
Beyond my body
And beyond this World

I am not the One
But I have somehow
Joined the One

I have become
As a god among men

I have entered
And now reside within
The Kingdom of Heaven
Even now
While still on earth

I am still *in* this World
And can still enjoy
The pleasures it offers
But I am no longer *of* this World

If you are able
Please hear this message well

I used to pray
For personal gain-
I used to pray

For money and objects,
For fame and for fortune

But now I have
Only one prayer,
I have
Only one desire-
And that is to remain forever
In this state of knowledge

This is all I want

I care for nothing else
But to never forget
That which I now know

Gold? Silver? Riches?
Fame? Fortune?
These things are as nothing-
They are as dirt
To what I have found

I have been born again!
I have returned home!
I am saved!

With a brimming heart
I wish you Peace
And Light
And Love
And the Great Rememberance
As well

CONSIDER READING NEXT

Consider continuing the Egyptian Enlightenment Series:
Author page: amazon.com/author/matthewbarnes
- The Emerald Tablet 101: book 1.
- The Hermetica 101: book 2.
- The Kybalion 101: book 3.

Matthew's "Zennish Series" books can be read in any order, but Matthew meant for them to be read in the following order:
- Tao Te Ching 101
- Albert Einstein, Zen Master
- Tao Te Ching 201
- Jesus Christ, Zen Master
- Dr. Seuss, Zen Master

I may also be adding to the Hindu Enlightenment series. Check my author page for progress: amazon.com/author/matthewbarnes
- The Bhagavad Gita

Or consider one of MS Barnes' novels:
- Folie¿
- Meet Frank King

*Be warned that Matt's novels are not the same as his spiritual works, though they do dive heavily into the power of the mind.

REFERENCES

Over the years, I have read many different versions of the Hermetica, from online versions to regular books. I have read scholarly approaches, and I have read more down-to-earth approaches.

My two favorite versions of the Hermetica, and the two that I have used for the most part to organize my own version include "The Hermetica: The Lost Wisdom of the Pharaohs" by Timothy Freke and Peter Gandy and "The Way of Hermes" by Clement Salaman, Dorine van Oyen, William D. Wharton and Jean-Pierre Mahe.

The topics in the original writings of the Hermetica are fairly scattered. It is hard to get an overall feel for any particular subject because that subject is talked about in bits and pieces in so many different places.

What Freke and Gandy's version did, and I can't even imagine the amount of time, understanding and effort this must have taken, was to take the wide range of subjects and topics that were scattered throughout the Hermetica and clump them together into coherent chapters, each chapter based on a single topic. This made the Hermetica infinitely easier to get a grasp on.

"The Way of Hermes" was a bit more scholarly, but included

a few areas not touched on in Freke and Gandy's version that I liked very much.

If you want more information on the Hermetica, I highly recommend either or both of these books.

As with my other works, what I am after is the "Big Picture". In a nutshell, and in modern terms and ideas, what is the Hermetica really trying to say? This is what I tried to convey in this book- my understanding of what the Hermetica is really trying to say.

As usual, I didn't follow each translation strictly, trying to say exactly what Hermes said, but instead tried to express what I felt he was trying to get across.

Our times and Hermes' time are very different. I was trying to give you the feeling and spirit of what I feel he meant, without being technical at all in preserving his original words.

AUTHOR BIO

Matthew Barnes is an avid learner who spent his early years in North Carolina. He was born in Greenville, NC and has lived in New Bern, Roanoke Rapids, Henderson (where he spent most of his childhood) and Raleigh, where he attended the University of North Carolina State. After obtaining degrees in Biochemistry and Chemistry, he attended Chiropractic School in Marietta, Georgia, where he graduated third in his class. Since that time, he has studied acupuncture and Chinese medicine, and settled down in rural Tennessee with his wife, 3 cats, 4 dogs, a crazy mother-in-law and a partridge in a pear tree. He has been in Tennessee for over 20 years now.

His main interests are learning, exploring, exercising and writing. Most of his works so far have been on spiritual-type themes, though he has also written a book on self-investing- another one of his hobbies.

To check the progress on his other works, go to:

http://www.amazon.com/Matthew-S.Barnes/e/B00SDYKSZ2

Made in United States
North Haven, CT
28 January 2024

48021940R00128